I0802127

IMAGES
of America

LAUGHLIN AIR FORCE BASE

This is an aerial shot of Laughlin Air Force Base in 1971, the year before the arrival of the 47th Flying Training Wing. One sees residential homes along the bottom of the image, mostly office and support structures in the center—above the track and field—with hangars and the airfield just beyond, toward the top of the picture. Southwestern Texas ranchland and scrub carry far into the distance. (Courtesy of the 47th Flying Training Wing History Office.)

On the Cover: The cover depicts a retreat ceremony prior to the graduation of undergraduate pilot training Class 87-02. This class of newly minted US Air Force pilots graduated from Laughlin Air Force Base on December 19, 1986. (Courtesy of the 47th Flying Training Wing History Office.)

IMAGES
of America

LAUGHLIN AIR FORCE BASE

Robert Thomas Marcell

ARCADIA
PUBLISHING

ISBN 978-1-4671-0709-9

Published by Arcadia Publishing
Charleston, South Carolina

Printed in the United States of America

Library of Congress Control Number: 2021933337

For all general information, please contact Arcadia Publishing:
Telephone 843-853-2070
Fax 843-853-0044
E-mail sales@arcadiapublishing.com
For customer service and orders:
Toll-Free 1-888-313-2665

Visit us on the Internet at www.arcadiapublishing.com

To the men and women of Laughlin Air Force Base—past, present, and future—for selflessly serving our nation and each other

Contents

ACKNOWLEDGMENTS

I would like to acknowledge that no man is an island, and no book is written alone. This book in particular is heavily informed by the work of dozens of professional Air Force historians, whose careful research over the years has helped to preserve the stories of Laughlin Air Force Base. Without their tireless efforts, much would be lost to the passage of time. I, personally, owe a great debt of gratitude to the historians at the Air Education and Training Command History Office, whose careful and continual guidance has helped to shape me into the historian I am today. These skilled and patient advisors include Gary W. Boyd, John M. "J.B." Baker, Patricia E. "Pat" Parrish, Joe B. Orr, and William A. "Bill" Manchester. Thanks are also due to 56th Fighter Wing historian Richard H. Griset Jr. for his advice on this book. I, too, would like to thank the assiduous lore keepers at the Laughlin Heritage Foundation for their decades of work in preserving the story of Laughlin: James S. "Jim" Long, US Air Force Lt. Col. (Ret.) Edward "Ed" Hanson, and Katherine A. Nielander in particular. Jim Long, specifically, helped review this material and offered helpful corrections and suggestions. Finally, thanks are owed to the 47th Judge Advocate Office for its legal guidance, Maj. Peter F. Havern in particular, as well as to the 47th Public Affairs Office for its security review of this material. Special thanks to Joel Langton for personally reviewing a draft of this book and offering many helpful suggestions.

I must also thank the staff at Arcadia Publishing for their invitation to write this book—and for their help along the road from "fun idea" to "finished manuscript." As a working historian, I value everyone with this organization for their work in preserving the local, regional, and national stories of the United States. Being a former park ranger, I have seen their familiar sepia-toned covers on many a bookshelf across our nation's most special places. In particular, though, I owe thanks to Arcadia Publishing's Lindsey L. Givens for approaching me about this book in the first place and to my editor at Arcadia, Angel Prohaska: thank you for your help, reminders, and maybe occasional arm twisting to keep me on task.

Having seen firsthand the dedication of the citizens of Del Rio, Texas, to the success of Laughlin Air Force Base and the US Air Force, I, too, would thank them. My admiration and appreciation are similarly due to the men and women—uniformed, contract, civil service, and their family members—who make Laughlin Air Force Base all that it is. Last, but certainly not least, I owe great personal thanks to my friends, mentors, and family for always believing in and encouraging me. The fact that there are too many of you to list here is the greatest blessing of my life.

With all of my thanks aside, I must, at this point, also acknowledge that any and all errors that one might find within this book are mine and mine alone.

Unless otherwise noted, all of the images in this volume are US Air Force photographs in the public domain. They can be found primarily in Laughlin Air Force Base's 47th Flying Training Wing History Office collection.

The views expressed in this book are those of the author and do not reflect the official policy or position of the US Air Force, US Department of Defense (DoD), or the US government. The appearance of DoD visual information does not imply or constitute DoD endorsement.

Introduction

Today, Laughlin Air Force Base is the largest producer of Air Force pilots in the US Air Force—and possibly the world. Specifically, Laughlin is the Air Force's largest Undergraduate Pilot Training (UPT) school. What that means is that Laughlin plays a large role in preparing the Air Force's next generation of military pilots for their combat missions across the world, training more of these pilots than any other pilot training base in the country. When young pilots come to Laughlin, often just or very shortly after receiving their commissions as officers of the US Air Force, they generally do not already know how to fly an airplane very well. The academic, practical, and technical skills that they learn at the base enable them first to become military pilots and then to specialize in either bomber and fighter-type aircraft or tanker and airlift-type aircraft. A few even go on to fly helicopters. Graduating from Undergraduate Pilot Training and "earning one's wings" is the first, critical step on every military aviator's path to the skies. And, in truth, Laughlin's proud tradition of training pilots goes back to the very beginning of the Laughlin story.

The base that is today Laughlin Air Force Base was originally proposed in the spring of 1942, shortly after Japan's attack on Pearl Harbor and America's entry into World War II. The citizens of Del Rio, Texas, approached the War Department and expressed their desire to do their part in supporting the war effort by inviting the Army to their community to build an air base. After Army Air Forces officials had had a chance to visit and survey the location, it was decided that they would indeed open an airfield just east of Del Rio, and construction began that very summer. By the end of 1942, the base was charged with a transition flying training mission—specifically, it was given the job of teaching existing Army Air Forces pilots how to fly the then new B-26 Marauder. This was no easy task, for this notorious bomber was so technically difficult on takeoffs and landings that it was originally nicknamed the "Widowmaker." In March 1943, the Army Air Forces base at Del Rio was officially given its own name, Laughlin Air Field, in honor of a bomber pilot from Del Rio—2nd Lt. Jack Thomas Laughlin—who was killed in action over the Pacific on January 29, 1942. After the war ended, Laughlin Air Field, like so many World War II military bases across the country, was closed down. This period of the base's history, from its opening in 1942 to its closure in 1945, is described in chapter one of this book.

Shortly after the Korean War started in 1950, the citizens of Del Rio once again fought for their base, with a delegation from the city making a very strong argument before Congress as to why Del Rio was the perfect spot for a flying base as they urged the newly minted US Air Force to reopen Laughlin as an Air Force base. The Air Force did just that, reviving the base in 1952 for the purpose of training fighter pilots for the war in Korea. Even after the war ended, the base continued training fighter pilots for a time, until the lack of suitable weapons ranges at Laughlin convinced the Air Force in 1955 to shift the base's training mission to combat crew training and pilot training. This brief rebuilding and wartime training period, and the short-lived change in mission that came after it, is covered in chapter two.

Chapter three is dedicated to the only non-training mission Laughlin Air Force Base has ever known. From 1957 to 1963, Laughlin was charged with a reconnaissance and weather mission, flying the Lockheed U-2 "Dragon Lady" spy plane. In this height–of–the–Cold War era, Laughlin played a key role in world history, for it was pilots from Laughlin's 4080th Strategic Wing that proved to the world that the Soviet Union was building nuclear missile sites in Cuba in 1962 in an attempt to counterbalance the missiles the United States had placed in Turkey. On October 14, 1962, Laughlin U-2 pilot Maj. Richard S. Heyser took the first pictures providing conclusive evidence of the Soviet missile buildup in Cuba, which kicked off a tense period of negotiation between the United States and the Union of Soviet Socialist Republics, which is now known as the Cuban Missile Crisis. It was probably the closest our world has ever come to an actual nuclear war between two nuclear-capable adversaries. Fortunately, cooler heads prevailed, and the Soviets withdrew their missiles from the island of Cuba following a more than monthlong standoff. The only combat casualty of the Cuban Missile Crisis—Maj. Rudolf Anderson Jr., who was shot down by a Cuban SA-2 Guideline surface-to-air missile—was also a Laughlin pilot. For giving his life in the line of duty, Major Anderson was posthumously awarded the first-ever Air Force Cross.

Chapter four discusses the coming of undergraduate pilot training to Laughlin Air Force Base in 1961. Until 1963, when the last U-2 flew off into Laughlin's horizon, the base was actually shared between two wings and two major commands—Strategic Air Command (SAC) and Air Training Command (ATC). Air Training Command's 3645th Pilot Training Wing, which was shortly after redesignated the 3646th Pilot Training Wing, was responsible for training new pilots at Laughlin from 1961 to 1972, at which time it was replaced by the 47th Flying Training Wing (47 FTW). The 47th Flying Training Wing has led training at Laughlin ever since. This period in the base's history is notable because it means that undergraduate pilot training has been the primary focus of the base ever since 1961, making it Laughlin's longest-lasting mission. It is through this mission that Laughlin Air Force Base has had a tremendous impact on the overall health of the Air Force as a whole.

Chapter five showcases the 47th Flying Training Wing from its activation in 1972 until 1994, when the Air Force entirely changed the way it taught undergraduate pilot training by shifting over to a specialized undergraduate pilot training, or SUPT, program. In SUPT, all pilots learn the basics of flying on a single aircraft (originally the T-37B Tweet and today the T-6A Texan II) before most specialize into either fighter/bombers (where they learn how to fly the T-38A, now T-38C, Talon) or tanker/airlifts (where they learn how to fly the T-1A Jayhawk). As noted, rather than tracking into fighter/bombers or tanker/airlifts, a few pilots go on to fly helicopters instead after learning the basics of flying in the T-6A Texan II. It was during this period, 1972–1994, that Laughlin adopted its present-day logo as well: The "XL." The year 1982 marked the 40th anniversary of the base's foundation, and the base celebrated by unveiling the XL symbol, with XL being the Roman numerals for 40. While originally intended to only last for the year, the XL logo (which of course is pronounced "excel") won the hearts and minds of base personnel, who today still refer to themselves as "Team XL." The base even started putting the XL on its planes—and today, anywhere in the world, a person can tell a Laughlin airplane from a non-Laughlin airplane by whether or not there's an XL on the plane's tail.

Finally, in concluding this portion of the narrative, chapter six examines Laughlin Air Force Base from the coming of SUPT to the present day, which includes stories about a devastating flood in 1998, the arrival of the T-6A Texan II aircraft, and a catastrophic 2016 hailstorm that set the wing back millions of dollars and thousands of hours in training, among other stories.

Chapter seven, the book's final chapter, departs from the timeline organization of chapters one through six and instead features some of the major heritage displays that can be found at Laughlin Air Force Base as well as a few of the base's named buildings and memorials. This chapter's highlights include photographs and descriptions of many of the airplanes that have been flown at Laughlin as part of its various training and reconnaissance missions. Laughlin Air Force Base has a beautiful air park with nine of these aircraft plus two additional static display aircraft at Ribas-Dominicci Plaza. It should be noted that some of the placards that go along with these displays have been pointed out to have inaccuracies, and the author has tried to identify these where he could in the captions.

Throughout this book, the author has tried to briefly, but completely, cover most of the significant events that have shaped Laughlin Air Force Base into the base that it is today. Unfortunately, some of the details and elaborations that might otherwise have been included have been left out in this book as necessitated by page and space requirements. The story of Laughlin covers nearly 80 years at this point, and the full story is far richer and deeper than could possibly be covered in a book of this length. Readers should, therefore, take this book to be an introduction to or a survey of the wonderful story of Laughlin Air Force Base. For those seeking more detail or a fuller telling of the story, the author would point them to the Laughlin Heritage Foundation Museum in Del Rio, Texas, and Laughlin Air Force Base's 47th Flying Training Wing History Office. The former is open to the public, and it is a fantastic resource for learning even more about any of the specific topics covered in this book. The latter is served by the 47th Flying Training Wing historian, who can also be a wonderful resource to researchers wanting to know more.

Altogether, Laughlin Air Force Base has trained thousands of pilots over the years. Many of these pilots have gone on to fly very significant military missions or to lead the Air Force itself in various capacities. Some Laughlin-trained pilots even return to Laughlin years later as group or wing commanders, leading the base that once taught them how to fly. This book covers many of the stories that all of these individuals played a part in shaping, likely learned of, or experienced directly. It is the author's hope that all who read the chapters ahead enjoy the story of Laughlin Air Force Base and come to admire the base and its people as much as he himself has come to admire them.

One

Laughlin Air Field 1942–1945

The US Army Air Forces announced its intention to build Laughlin Air Field outside of Del Rio, Texas, in April 1942. Construction began on July 2, 1942, and the base was ready for occupation by October 28, 1942.

Originally, Laughlin was planned to be a training base for advanced flying training, but on September 26, 1942, before the base was even ready for operations, the mission was changed to bombardier training. In December 1942, as preparations for flying were getting started, this mission again changed, and the station became a B-26 Marauder transition flying training school. This would be its mission for most of the war.

Laughlin got its name on March 3, 1943, when it was designated Laughlin Army Air Field. A little over three weeks later, on March 28, a commemoration naming ceremony was held so dedicating the base as Laughlin. Before it was Laughlin, the base was designated with much more cumbersome names. First, it was the United States Army Air Forces Bombardier School, Del Rio, Texas, and then it was the US Army Air Forces Transition Flying School, Medium Bombardment, near Del Rio, Texas.

Near the end of the war, in early 1945, transition training at Laughlin switched from training on the B-26 Marauder to training on the Douglas A-26 Invader. However, within days of the formal surrender of Japan on September 2, 1945, the announcement was made that Laughlin Army Air Field would close. The base was abandoned in October 1945, and the land, which the Army retained ownership of, was leased to local ranchers. This chapter explores the story of this period in the base's history.

The Air Force became its own branch of the military in September 1947—after World War II had ended. Before that, the air power of the United States was primarily managed by the US Army Air Forces, a branch of the US Army. In this photograph, Army officials visit Del Rio, Texas, at the site of what would become Laughlin Army Air Field.

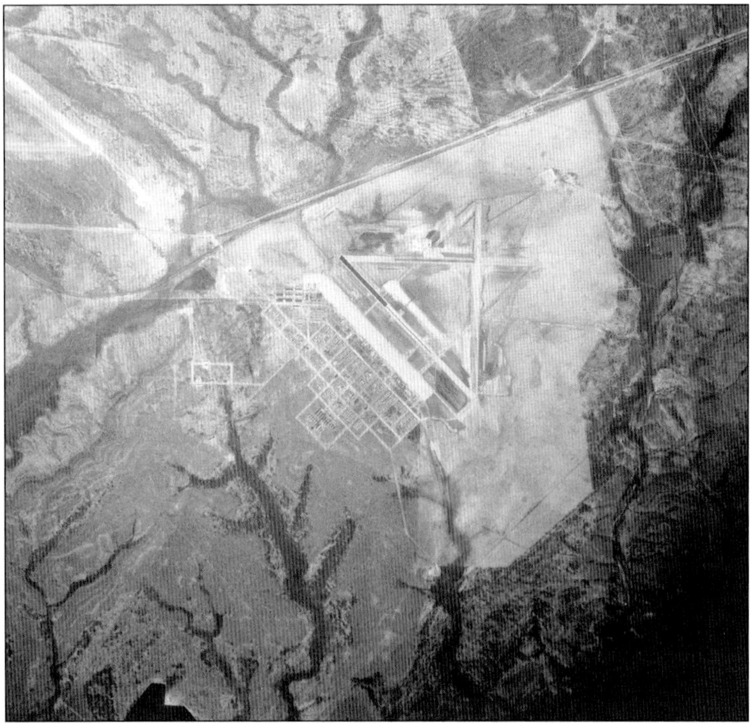

Construction began on the airfield in July 1942 and was completed by the end of that year. The process of establishing the airfield in Del Rio officially started May 4–5, 1942, when Army engineers formally agreed that a site seven miles east of Del Rio, Texas—which had been selected by the Del Rio Chamber of Commerce Aviation Committee—would indeed be acceptable for a flying school.

The United States Army Air Forces Bombardier School, Del Rio, Texas, was activated in September 1942. Its entire complement of troops consisted of 28 officers and enlisted men. Because construction was ongoing through the end of the year, military housing was in the city of Del Rio, not on the base proper. Indeed, for a time even the headquarters was in downtown Del Rio at the federal building.

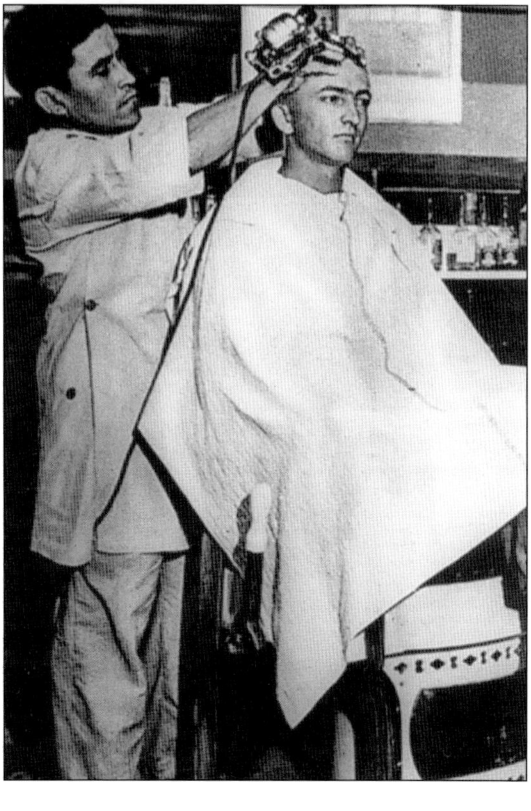

Before bombardier training could officially begin at the airfield, the base's mission was changed. This occurred in December 1942, when base leaders learned they would now be in charge of transition B-26 Marauder training. This meant that they would be taking already experienced pilots and teaching them how to fly on a new type of plane. Here, base personnel are being made base operations-ready too.

The first B-26 Marauders arrived at the US Army Air Forces Transition Flying School, Medium Bombardment, near Del Rio, Texas, in January 1943. The station even proudly claimed to possess the original B-26 airplane, nicknamed "Old Gran Pappy." In this photograph, a base maintenance crew looks inside of one of the new airplanes.

Transition pilot training in the B-26 began on February 1, 1943. Classes, comprised of pilots and copilots, were small and had irregular start dates. Training lasted about 4.5 weeks originally, then became more standardized at around nine. The first class of 22–23 students graduated on March 3, 1943. (The historical and public affairs notes differ on the subject of student count, with public affairs suggesting it was 22 students.)

In addition to being the date its first students graduated, March 3, 1943, was also the date that the training base received its official designation—Laughlin Army Air Field. This was in honor of a pilot from Del Rio named Jack Thomas Laughlin, who was killed in action over the Pacific. The base's naming ceremony would take place a few weeks later with a big event on March 28, 1943. This photograph shows the base's airfield with its fleet of B-26 Marauders. This airplane was called the "Widowmaker" by a few of the pilots who flew it due to the fact that it required some real technical skill to fly it. One of the difficulties was that its landing speeds were higher than the landing speeds of other aircraft that pilots at the time had trained on, so when they would approach the runway for a landing, the pilots would feel like they were coming in too fast, try to slow the airplane down, and then stall it, leading to a crash.

Second Lt. Jack Thomas Laughlin, for whom Laughlin Air Force Base is named and who is pictured here in his official portrait from 1941, was born in Del Rio, Texas, on September 17, 1914. He earned a bachelor's degree in business administration from the University of Texas in 1938 and worked for the University of Texas Museum until, in September 1940, he joined the Army Air Corps Aviation Cadet Program to achieve his dream of flying. After completing training at Santa Maria, Moffett, Mather, and Bakersfield Fields in California, Laughlin earned his wings at Stockton Field on April 27, 1941, and was assigned to a B-17 bombardment mission. While in California, Laughlin met Mary Fundulakis of Sacramento, California, and the two married at the Fort Douglas chapel in August 1941. Shortly after the United States' entry into World War II, Laughlin lost his life on January 29, 1942, when his B-17 (tail number 41-2476) was shot down by Japanese fighters during a bombing raid over the Makassar Strait near Borneo. It was likely Laughlin's first combat mission.

Second Lieutenant Laughlin's life was celebrated at a grand naming ceremony at Laughlin Army Air Field on March 28, 1943. Pictured here speaking at the podium at this event is Maj. Gen. Gerald Clark Brant—at that time the commander of the Gulf Coast Army Air Forces Training Center, Randolph Field, Texas. The woman just behind him, looking toward the camera, is Jack Laughlin's widow, Mary Laughlin.

Another image from the Laughlin Army Air Field naming ceremony gives a better indication of the size of the crowd in attendance, mostly from the base and from nearby Del Rio, Texas. A full military band was present, and after the speeches and dedication, people were allowed to mingle and to share memories and stories with one another.

Del Rio, Texas, is right along the border with Mexico in south-central, southwestern Texas, and it is very often a land of bright sunlight and unyielding heat. The clear, warm weather makes it ideal for flying training but sometimes uncomfortable for living. In this picture, crowds attending the March 28, 1943, Laughlin naming ceremony seek refuge from the sun beneath one of the field's B-26 Marauders.

In attendance at the March 28, 1943, naming ceremony with Mary Laughlin—pictured far right—were her family and the family of 2nd Lt. Jack Thomas Laughlin. Carried in Mary's arms is Jacki Laughlin, her daughter with Jack Laughlin, who was born on August 14, 1942. Because 2nd Lt. Jack Thomas Laughlin died in January 1942, he never got to meet his daughter.

After the ceremonies, Mary and Jacki Laughlin met with Major General Brant and Laughlin Army Air Field's commander, Col. George W. Mundy. Newly named colonel, Mundy was the first "operational" commander of the base, overseeing the base's actual training mission, though Col. Edward W. Suarez was the very first base commander overall, having been charged with overseeing the construction of the base and its preparation originally for bombardier training. Col. Emmett F. Yost would take command of the base on June 20, 1944, and Col. Joseph C. O'Neal would have the command for the base's closure, from September 8 to October 30, 1945. After Laughlin reopened in 1952, becoming Laughlin Air Force Base, Mary and her daughter would remain close friends with people at the base that was named after their late husband and father.

More than 64 years after the March 28, 1943, naming ceremony, from August 15 to 17, 2007, Jacki Laughlin—now Jacki Laughlin Mitchell—visited the base again with her own daughter, Holly, pictured here with then wing commander Col. Mike Minahan. They stand before Laughlin's central flagpole, where a plaque memorializing 2nd Lt. Jack Thomas Laughlin can be found to this day. Jacki passed in 2016 and perhaps finally got to meet her father.

By the end of 1943, Laughlin Army Air Field training consisted of both flying and ground school training, and the base was producing large classes of Marauder pilots. They had four groups of officer flight instructors comprised of about 60–65 instructors and a host of supporting services. Pictured here is Col. Emmett F. Yost, who would command the base from June 20, 1944, to September 7, 1945.

Numerous buildings served the airfield and its population during the war years. Pictured here is the commissary, where soldiers could purchase groceries. There was also a post office, theater, recreation hall, mess hall, and PX (or post exchange) where soldiers could buy more retail-like consumer goods and services as opposed to the victuals they would find at the commissary.

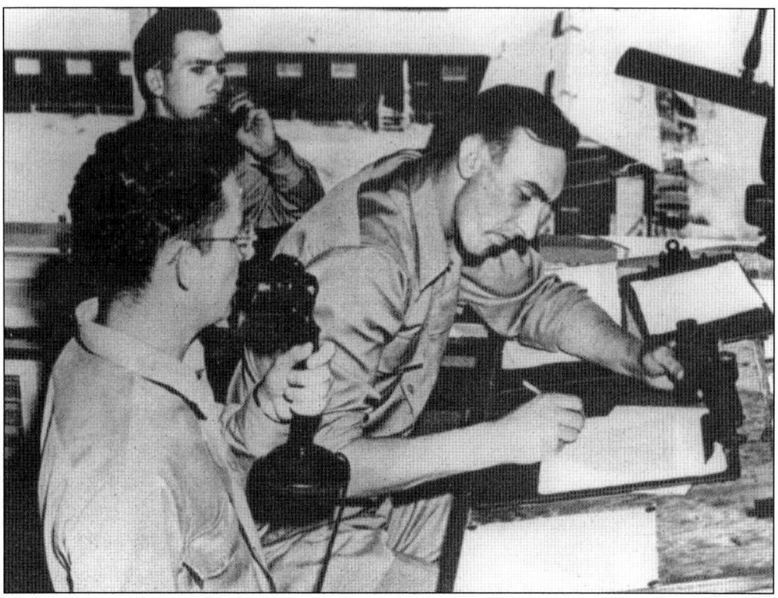

This image of Laughlin Army Air Field control tower personnel gives one an idea of how airplanes were directed back before the high-tech electronics of today. By the end of Laughlin Army Air Field's life as an Army airfield, it was a bustling base with plenty of air traffic for the controllers to manage.

HEADQUARTERS
ARMY AIR FORCES PILOT SCHOOL
(SPECIALIZED TWO-ENGINE)

Laughlin Army Air Field

DEL RIO, TEXAS

★

To the Personnel of Laughlin Army Air Field:

Through the portals of Laughlin Field have passed many young student officers destined to play important roles in the struggle of the United Nations to bring peace again to the world.

Our primary job has been that of teaching these student officers how to fly the B-26, or Martin Marauder, airplane under any kind of condition. That we have succeeded is attested to by reports from the Theaters of War which laud the battle prowess of the B-26 and the bravery and dexterity of the pilots and crews.

When the history of this war is written, it is likely that the exploits of the B-26 will form an interesting chapter. Every member of this command can then feel that he has had a definite part in the achievement, for it has been the combination of hundreds of jobs, well-accomplished, that has made possible the turning out of finished B-26 pilots.

To all those who have given of their best toward this end, I extend my commendations.

The final victory—although it is in sight—is not yet won. Therefore, it is necessary for all members of this command to stretch their abilities to the utmost in the months to come, to give freely of their time and talents toward the achievement of our ultimate goals: victory and peace.

George W. Mundy.

Colonel, Air Corps
Commanding

This letter, published in the 1943 Laughlin Army Air Field yearbook, was penned by then base commander Col. George W. Mundy to his troops. Despite Colonel Mundy's high hopes that "the final victory" was in sight, World War II would last two more years and would cost between 400,000 and 420,000 American lives. Laughlin would transition to training on a new plane near the very end of its service, the A-26 Invader, and would also suffer a devastating fire on August 27, 1945, which locals at the time believed was a contributing factor in the Army's decision to close the base. Nevertheless, the men and women of Laughlin Army Air Field gave their all during the three-year period between 1942 when the base opened and 1945 when the base was closed, ultimately graduating 2,924 B-26 pilots. Although the airfield did not survive the war as an Army base, it was just the beginning of things to come for Laughlin and Del Rio, for Laughlin would soon be reborn again under the newly minted US Air Force.

Two

Laughlin Air Force Base 1952–1957

The end of World War II did not bring with it an end to war. Tensions began building between the United States and the Soviet Union (USSR) almost immediately, with the USSR shutting down land access to Berlin in 1948 (necessitating the massive Allied relief effort known as the Berlin Airlift) and then exploding its own atomic bomb in 1949. Also in 1949, China's Nationalist forces fell to Mao Zedong's Communists, and then, in 1950, Communist North Korea invaded South Korea. The United States intervened in this latter conflict, feeling that the spread of Communism, left unchecked, was a direct threat to the American way of life—and thus began the Korean War (1950–1953).

It was in this climate that the citizens of Del Rio asked the US government to rebuild Laughlin, sending a committee to Washington with reams of weather data and statistics to make their argument for doing so. Their argument was persuasive, and in 1952, the land was given to the newly fashioned US Air Force. The base, by then just a couple of overgrown runways, was placed on active status in May 1952. Laughlin was given to Air Training Command (ATC), which subsequently assigned it to the Flying Training Air Force.

ATC established the 3645th Pilot Training Wing at Laughlin—no longer Laughlin Field but Laughlin Air Force Base—with the idea being that it would provide basic instruction in single-engine aircraft for US military aviators and for pilots from Allied countries. In October 1952, before this training had even begun, ATC transferred the base to the Crew Training Air Force instead and redesignated the wing as the 3645th Flying Training Wing (Fighter).

The mission of newly rebuilt Laughlin would be, in this era, to train fighter pilots in the T-33 Shooting Star, the F-80 Shooting Star, and the F-84 Thunderjet. Base personnel hit the ground running, even before reconstruction was fully completed—Laughlin's air traffic controllers had to improvise without a control tower, for example, making do with a parked C-47 on the ramp as their "tower" for a few months—and life at Laughlin began anew.

Laughlin Air Force Base had to be rebuilt nearly from the ground up. The area had been left to the goats, quite literally, with local goat ranchers using it as range land until the military's return. Nonetheless, in this aerial view of the base from 1953, one can still see the original footprint into which Laughlin was rebuilt in 1952.

Laughlin's first class of 17 pilots under the new fighter pilot program started training on February 19, 1953. Although the base by this point had been reactivated nine months earlier, the delay from activation to training was due to reconstruction requirements as well as a lack of gunnery ranges, aircraft, and instructors. The lack of gunnery ranges would remain a problem for this entire period in the base's history.

One of the very first buildings reconstructed on base—which can still be found at Laughlin today, making it one of the oldest structures still standing—was the chapel. It was built in 1954. This picture was probably taken in 1961, and its modern-day annex was added to it in 1967.

On April 29, 1953, Laughlin's first class of jet fighter pilots completed their combat readiness fighter/bomber course. Students proceeded to Nellis Air Force Base, Nevada, or Luke Air Force Base, Arizona, for phase two of the course using the F-84 or F-86, respectively, then would be assigned to fly in the war until the armistice was signed on July 27, 1953. Col. Thomas L. Mosley, pictured here, was Laughlin's wing commander during the war.

By June 30, 1953, the base listed the following aircraft in its inventory: 42 T-33As, 28 F-80As, 36 F-80Bs, 1 F-80C, 8 F-84Ds, 4 T-6Ds, 3 TB-25Js, 2 C-45Gs, 2 TF-80As, 1 C-47D, and a L-5G. F-84Es were assigned to Laughlin in February 1954, but they were only used for a short time. Laughlin pilots primarily flew the T-33A Shooting Star, shown here in a photograph from 1964.

Laughlin's 1,000th fighter/bomber program pilot graduated with Class 54-D on April 16, 1954. With this class's graduation, the total number of pilots trained by the revived base had reached 1,085 in a little over one year of training. Pictured here is formation flying in several of the T-33 Shooting Stars flown at Laughlin from 1953 to 1958 (and again from 1961 to 1965). This photograph is from 1955.

On April 30, 1954, Laughlin Air Force Base got its own railroad. It consisted of one engine, one mile of track, and no cars. It also carried no passengers. Operated by one military and one civilian trainman, engine No. 1238's job was to pick up boxcars from where it connected with commercial rail and transport them to Base Supply for unloading into supply tents like the one pictured here.

The peak of combat crew training at Laughlin Air Force Base was reached in May 1954. The 3645th Flying Training Wing (Fighter) was training 377 students at that time, and between them, students and instructors flew a total of 9,175 hours that month. The base's population, not counting students who were only there temporarily, had reached 3,191 people. Pictured are some of the 3645th's firefighters.

In late June 1954, Laughlin and Del Rio suffered a flood resulting from the remnants of Hurricane Alice, which moved through the local area before dying down near Big Bend National Park on June 27, 1954. The region around Del Rio saw over 30 inches of rainfall, flooding the Rio Grande and the surrounding area. This photograph is from Laughlin's flooded airfield.

A few months after the flood, on August 24, 1954, Laughlin Air Force Base and the city of Del Rio received welcome news—Laughlin was designated a permanent Air Force installation. This time, the end of the war did not mean the end of Laughlin. Pictured here from 1957 is the base headquarters building.

In the fall of 1954, the 3645th Flying Training Wing (Fighter) was redesignated as the 3645th Combat Crew Training Wing (Fighter). In addition to pilots and students, however, the base also needed a vast support team to ensure that the training could continue safely and unhindered at all times. Pictured here is one of the base ambulances with a driver.

In May 1955, Laughlin reached peak population since its reactivation. Total onsite population, not counting students, was at 3,495. The total population, including detached personnel, was 3,776 people. This photograph from the era offers a look into another important support role in maintaining so many people on a military base—feeding them all!

On September 1, 1955, Laughlin transferred from a combat crew training wing (fighter) back to a flying training wing (fighter). This time its mission was teaching basic, single-engine pilot training in the T-33. The first class of students arrived from Williams Air Force Base in Arizona, and from the start of basic fighter gunnery training in February 1953 to August 1955, Laughlin successfully trained 3,429 student officers. Of this, 1,879 were US Air Force or Air National Guard

officers, while 1,550 were Allied nationals. To accomplish this mission, students, instructors, and training supervisors flew 162,000 hours. With the exception of 1,900 hours flown by instructors in the F-84 during the spring of 1954, flying hours represented T-33 flying time. The F-84 flying was in anticipation of the discontinuation of the split-phase system of training, but the plan did not materialize. Pictured is Laughlin's front gate in 1957.

On November 1, 1955, ATC headquarters at Scott Air Force Base in Illinois announced that jurisdiction, control, and accountability of the Eagle Pass Auxiliary Field in Eagle Pass, Texas, was transferred from Laredo Air Force Base to Laughlin Air Force Base, growing the young base's responsibilities. This photograph is of the Eagle Pass Auxiliary Field in 1986.

On December 7, 1955, single-engine training for basic pilots began when the first class of aviation cadets entered the course. Laughlin Air Force Base and Williams Air Force Base had essentially exchanged missions. Williams Air Force Base's basic pilot mission was brought to Laughlin, and Laughlin's crew training mission was reestablished at the Arizona site in early 1956. Aircraft, instructors, and know-how were exchanged, facilitating the transition. Pictured is Laughlin's operations building for pilot training in 1954.

On December 20, 1955, the last combat crew fighter training phase I class graduated from Laughlin. Pictured is Col. Samuel C. Gurney Jr., who was Laughlin's wing commander from August 1, 1955, until the termination of its training mission in March 1957. From 1956 onward, Laughlin's mission would be basic pilot training.

On January 1, 1956, the 3645th Combat Crew Training Wing (Fighter) was officially redesignated the 3645th Pilot Training Wing (Basic Single Engine) by General Order No. 52, issued on December 14, 1955. Training continued in the T-33 aircraft, but the curriculum changed to reflect the new material. In this photograph are the base flagpole and headquarters building.

In July 1956, peak load of basic single-engine training was reached with 408 students. A total of 8,972 hours were flown by students and instructors that month. This photograph captures one class of these students, Class 57-C. From left to right are 2nd Lt. Donald J. Holtz, 2nd Lt. Hugo E. Quiroga (from Chile), 2nd Lt. Earnest A. Boehler Jr., 2nd Lt. Richard A. Denay, and 2nd Lt. Billy J. Cobb.

Earnest Boehler, from Class 57-C (at right), returned to Laughlin in 2007 to donate materials from his career. At the time, he noted how impressed he was with how much technology had changed flying training, commenting that in his day "we used grease pencils for log books and grade reports." In this photograph, Boehler presents one of his historical mementos to 47th Flying Training Wing vice commander Col. Dan Laro Clark.

On October 28, 1956, this plaque was given to Laughlin by the Belgian government in thanks for training dozens of Belgian Air Force pilots since 1952. It was attached to Laughlin's main flagpole, where it can still be found today. It carries the coat of arms of the Belgian royal family and is inscribed in Belgium's official languages: French and Flemish. It reads: "In recognition of services rendered to Belgian military students."

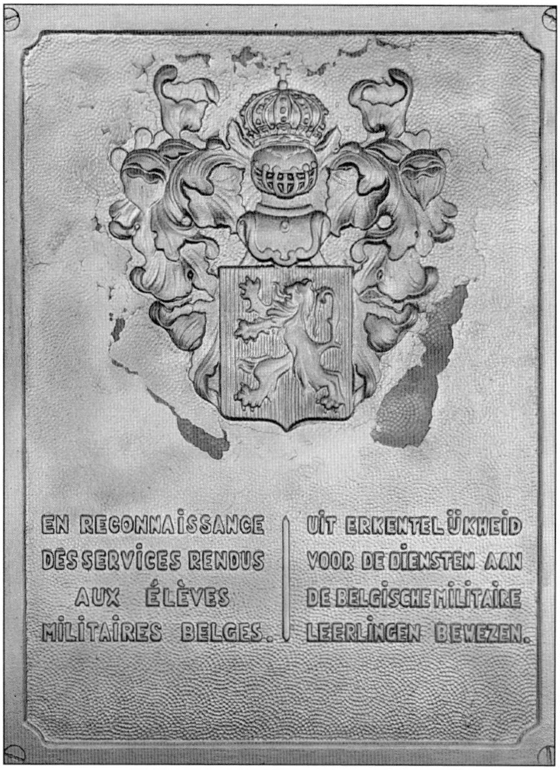

In November 1956, news was released to the press that control of Laughlin Air Force Base would be transferring to the Second Air Force, Strategic Air Command, on April 1, 1957. Laughlin's new mission was to be high-altitude weather reconnaissance conducted in RB-57 jet bombers. Laughlin's ATC mission was to be absorbed by other flying training Air Force bases. Pictured is the Laughlin hospital in 1957.

By May 15, 1957, all Air Training Command activity at Laughlin Air Force Base had ended. The very last basic single-engine class completed training on April 13, 1957; graduated on April 27, 1957; and departed to careers elsewhere in the Air Force. This resulted in the inactivation of the 3645th Pilot Training Wing, and Laughlin Air Force Base was, for the first and (so far) only time in its history, not a training base. Its new mission would be a reconnaissance one, and its new caretakers would be the 4080th Strategic Reconnaissance Wing, Light. In this photograph from 1954, the American flag is being lowered during the end of day retreat—an important daily routine and ceremony on military bases across the nation and around the world. But while Air Training Command's leaving represented an end of an era at Laughlin, the new wing would accomplish great things at the base and would even go on to shape world history.

Three

The Spy Plane Years 1957–1963

Laughlin made world history in October 1962 for the crucial role its pilots played in the Cuban Missile Crisis. It was Laughlin fliers who took the pictures that proved to the world that the Soviet Union was building and arming missile sites in Cuba. Laughlin was positioned to play a role in this enormously significant event in 1957, when the base was transferred into the control of Strategic Air Command (SAC) and assigned to the 4080th Strategic Reconnaissance Wing, Light, coming in from Turner Air Force Base, Georgia.

The 4080th Strategic Reconnaissance Wing flew the Lockheed U-2 Dragon Lady spy plane and the RB-57D Canberra. It deployed aircraft and personnel around the world as part of its Cold War–era reconnaissance mission and also provided high-altitude meteorological data for operational weather forecasting. In addition to these primary responsibilities in recon and weather, the wing also conducted signal and electronic intelligence flights and collected air samples from aboveground nuclear tests. On June 15, 1960, the 4080th Strategic Reconnaissance Wing, Light, was redesignated the 4080th Strategic Wing.

The Air Force assumed the role of high-altitude reconnaissance missions from the Central Intelligence Agency (CIA) in October 1962, just in time for Maj. Richard S. Heyser to capture the critical photographs showing the Soviet missile buildup in Cuba, which were taken on October 14, 1962. During the month of October, a number of spy flights were flown over Cuba to gather data on this buildup, and the only combat casualty of the 1962 Cuban Missile Crisis came on October 27, 1962, when Maj. Rudolf Anderson Jr. was shot down by an SA-2 Guideline surface-to-air missile on one of these flights. Today, the flying student building and main assembly hall at Laughlin Air Force Base is named Anderson Hall in his honor.

This chapter looks at this short, but eventful, period in Laughlin's history, with the coming and leaving of the 4080th Strategic Wing.

Coming into Laughlin on April 1, 1957, the 4080th Strategic Reconnaissance Wing, Light, flew the U-2 Dragon Lady and the RB-57D Canberra, pictured here. The first U-2 arrived on base on June 11, 1957, and the first RB-57 was added to the 4080th in July 1957. Both of these aircraft were reconnaissance and weather data collection airplanes.

Col. Hubert Zemke, pictured here, was the first commander of the 4080th Strategic Reconnaissance Wing, Light, and helped bring the wing to Laughlin. Zemke was a noteworthy commander in his own right, and his 56th Fighter Group in World War II came to be known as "Zemke's Wolf Pack." He served as the 4080th's commander from April 1957 to November 1957, when the role was turned over to Brig. Gen. Austin J. Russell.

The U-2 Dragon Lady, an example of which is pictured here, was the primary aircraft of the 4080th Strategic Reconnaissance Wing, Light, and later the 4080th Strategic Wing. This spy plane is still in use today, more than a half-century later. As a high-altitude, long-distance flier, it has no equal, and it played a vital role in the intelligence missions of the Cold War.

In April 1958, not long after the 4080th's arrival, construction began on the 500-unit Capehart Housing Project. The goal was to provide expanded on-base housing for permanent residents. Streets on base were named in honor of leaders in aviation or in memory of outstanding cadets assigned to Laughlin who had lost their lives in training missions. Bowling Street, pictured here, was named after 1st Lt. James R. Bowling.

The first family to move into the new housing units was Master Sergeant and Mrs. Gendron with their son, pictured at left at the ribbon-cutting ceremony. The photograph below shows the ribbon cutting with a number of important dignitaries from both on base and off base. From left to right are Jack Hosley, Col. A.J. Bratton (the 4080th Strategic Reconnaissance Wing commander from December 17, 1958, to July 27, 1960), Phil Ricks (for whom Ricks Hall, one of the dormitories on base, was later named), Manuel Arravaga Jr., Mrs. Gendron and son, Major Hobkius, Master Sergeant Gendron, John L. Rodson, Del Rio mayor A.C. Kennedy, and three unidentified men.

On August 18, 1959, a noncomissioned officer preparatory school was established at Laughlin to assist with the development of enlisted leaders. The photograph here is of one of Laughlin's entry gates from this time period. In the upper left of the sign is the emblem of Strategic Air Command.

The motto of Strategic Air Command was "Peace is Our Profession." That motto is displayed prominently in this picture from the same time period as the previous image. Also on display here is the emblem and patch design of the 4080th Strategic Reconnaissance Wing—the emblem on the right with the knight and the dragon.

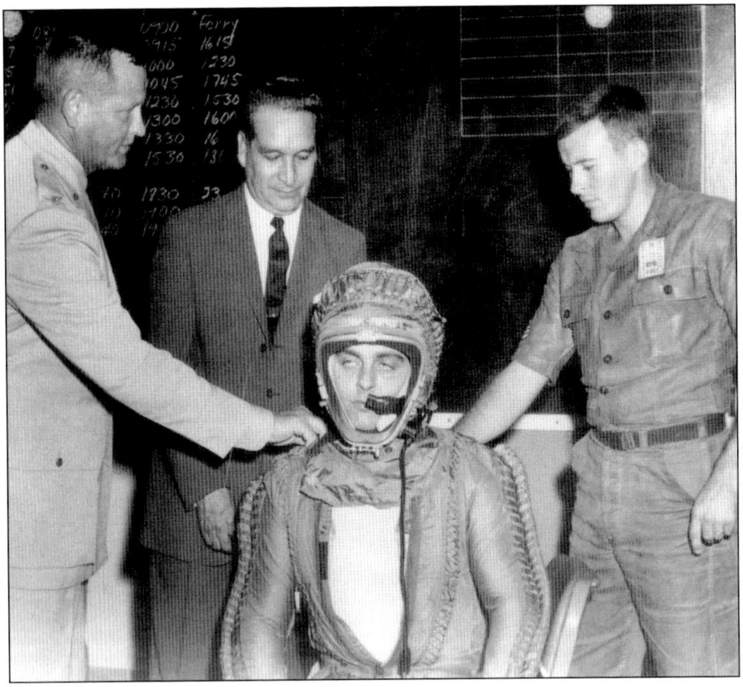

On June 15, 1960, Strategic Air Command inactivated the 4080th's 4025th Strategic Reconnaissance Squadron. This squadron flew RB-57 Canberras, so these aircraft were afterwards sent to other squadrons across the Air Force or deposited at the Air Force storage depot at Davis-Monthan Air Force Base in Arizona. After that, only U-2s were flown by the 4080th, which required pressure suits like the one pictured here during a fitting.

Pres. Dwight D. Eisenhower and Secretary of State Christian Herter visited Laughlin on October 24, 1960. They met in Del Rio with Mexican president López Mateos. The pair signed a treaty to construct Amistad Dam on the Rio Grande, sealing it with an impromptu hug. This embrace inspired Del Rio's annual *abrazo* ceremony, where leaders from Del Rio and Acuña, Mexico, embrace one another as neighbors. (Courtesy of the Laughlin Heritage Foundation's Strot Collection.)

On January 9, 1961, Clarence L. "Kelly" Johnson, chief designer of the U-2, visited Laughlin Air Force Base. He was joined on this visit by Robert Shumaker, U-2 aircraft test pilot; Glen Fulkerson, flight test engineer; and Art Bradley and Art Verick of the Lockheed Corporation. This photograph shows Kelly Johnson with U-2 pilot Francis Gary Powers (right) in 1966. (Courtesy of the National Museum of the United States Air Force.)

It was announced on March 30, 1961, that Laughlin would be one of 52 bases across the world that would be closing, and the 4080th began planning to move to Davis-Monthan Air Force Base. Fortunately for the base and for the people of Del Rio, this would not come to pass. Pictured here is an image from a 1961 Laughlin Air Force Base Appreciation Days event. The young woman is Debbie Foster.

On July 31, 1961, the base received word that its closure was to be postponed; however, it would thenceforth be shared between Strategic Air Command (SAC) and Air Training Command (ATC), as Laughlin would be absorbing a portion of the Undergraduate Pilot Training (UPT) program from the closing of Laredo Air Force Base. This picture from July 1, 1961, shows the change of command ceremony of the 4080th Strategic Wing. From left to right are Val Verde County judge Jim Lindsey, Gilbert Murray, Col. John A. Des Portes, and Col. William J. Wilcox. Col. John A. Des Portes was taking command of the 4080th, and he would be the last commander of the 4080th Strategic Wing at Laughlin Air Force Base.

As the 4080th Strategic Wing continued preparing for an eventual move to Davis-Monthan (which had not been canceled), command jurisdiction of Laughlin Air Force Base transferred from SAC to ATC on April 1, 1962. The 4080th was notified that it should be prepared to move by or around July 1963. However, there was one more major event at Laughlin before it went. Pictured here is the Laughlin Fiesta Center in 1960.

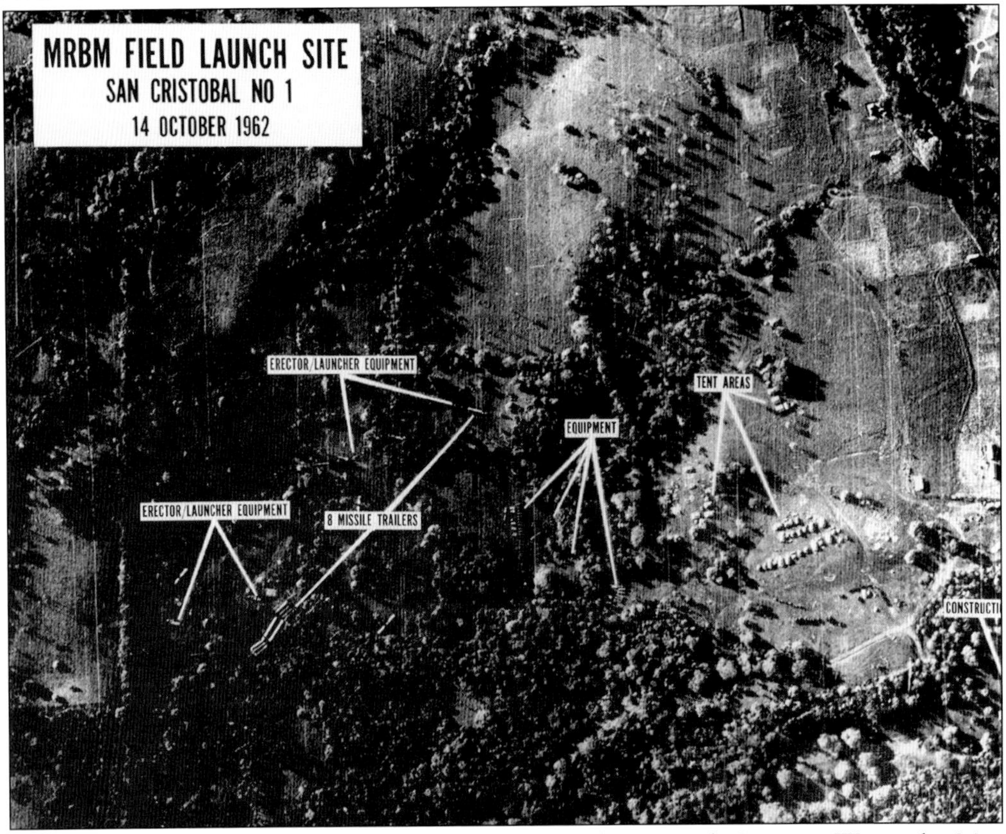

On October 14, 1962, Laughlin entered world history when 4080th Strategic Wing pilot Maj. Richard S. Heyser obtained the first conclusive evidence that the Soviet Union was building and arming missile sites in Cuba. These were intended by the Soviet Union to threaten the United States in the same way that the US missiles positioned in Turkey threatened Russia. In this image, one of these missile buildup sites is pictured. (Courtesy of the John F. Kennedy Presidential Library and Museum, Boston.)

Maj. Richard S. Heyser's critical photographic evidence of the missile buildup efforts in Cuba naturally inspired many more U-2 flights over Cuba, which very shortly followed. After one of these flyovers, which occurred on October 27, 1962, Maj. Rudolf Anderson Jr., a pilot of the 4080th's 4028th Strategic Reconnaissance Weather Squadron, pictured here, failed to make it home and was declared missing in action. It was later determined that a SA-2 Guideline surface-to-air missile from Cuba struck his U-2 and caused his death. Major Anderson was born in Spartanburg, South Carolina, on September 15, 1927, and he joined the US Air Force in 1951. Over the course of his Air Force career leading up to the Cuban Missile Crisis, he earned multiple medals and honors for his reconnaissance missions, and he was admired as a talented and dedicated pilot. His remains were returned to the United States in early November 1962.

On November 7, 1962, Maj. Rudolf Anderson Jr. was buried with full military honors in a closed-casket ceremony in Greenville, South Carolina. Major Anderson was the only combat casualty of the 1962 Cuban Missile Crisis. Today, Laughlin Air Force Base's Anderson Hall training complex is named in his honor. Outside of this building's main assembly hall, one can find a U-2 pilot partial pressure suit on display.

Here, Pres. John F. Kennedy pins an Air Force Outstanding Unit Award on the 4080th Strategic Wing's flag at a ceremony at Homestead Air Force Base in Florida on November 26, 1962. On July 12, 1963, Laughlin's last U-2s left for their new home in Arizona. From Laughlin Air Force Base, the 4080th had played a critical role in deterring nuclear war.

Four

Earning One's Wings 1961–1972

In 1961, the US Air Force announced that Laughlin would once again train pilots. Originally, the plan was for approximately one half of Laredo Air Force Base's undergraduate pilot student load to shift to Laughlin Air Force Base, but ultimately, Laredo would close down entirely and Laughlin would take over the mission.

In October 1961, Air Training Command (ATC) reactivated the 3645th Pilot Training Wing at Laughlin and began transferring 41 Cessna T-37 Tweets to the shared base (as the 4080th Strategic Wing was also still there at this time). On February 15, 1962, ATC redesignated the 3645th as the 3646th Pilot Training Wing. And on April 1, 1962, command of the base shifted from Strategic Air Command to ATC entirely, with the 4080th departing by the summer of 1963. From that point on, the base had a singular focus on training undergraduate pilots—a mission that it has continued to hold onto ever since.

The 1960s saw not only the rebirth of pilot training at Laughlin but also the appearance of three US presidents. These visits started with Pres. Dwight D. Eisenhower's 1960 trip to Laughlin (described on page 42) to sign a treaty with Mexican president Adolfo López Mateos in nearby Del Rio. This treaty called for the construction of the Amistad Dam (*amistad* means "friendship" in Spanish), a joint dam that was completed in 1969 and created the beautiful Amistad Reservoir Lake. Pres. Lyndon B. Johnson visited for the same reason (to discuss the progress of the dam) on December 3, 1966, and Pres. Richard M. Nixon's visit on September 8, 1969, was for the completed dam's dedication ceremony.

After this eventful decade, the 3646th Pilot Training Wing was inactivated in 1972. At that time, the Air Force was starting to get rid of its four-digit major command–controlled (or MAJCON) units and replacing them with official Air Force–created and –controlled wings instead. This process continued into the 1990s, making Laughlin's 3646th an early casualty of this important reorganization effort. So it was that in September 1972, the 47th Flying Training Wing would come to Laughlin, replacing the inactivating 3646th.

On October 16, 1961, Air Training Command activated the 3645th Pilot Training Wing at Laughlin Air Force Base. The brand-new wing only had two officers and three airmen assigned to it at this time. The first commander, pictured here, was Col. August F. Taute, who served as wing commander from October 31, 1961, to February 14, 1962.

Also on October 16, 1961, the newly activated 3645th was assigned its first T-37 Tweet, tail number 56-3564, which was transferred from Laredo Air Force Base to Laughlin Air Force Base. In all, Laughlin would receive 41 T-37Bs and 13 T-33As from Laredo, Sheppard, Moody, Vance, and James Connally Air Force Bases. Pictured in this photograph from 1964 is a row of T-37s.

On November 20, 1961, the first undergraduate pilot training class started at Laughlin Air Force Base. Twenty-three students were in this class, which was Class 63-D. In this aerial picture from 1963, one can see the state of the base as it was for most of the 1960s, with its residential housing in the south, office and support buildings in the center, and airfield at the top right.

On February 15, 1962, the 3645th Pilot Training Wing was redesignated the 3646th Pilot Training Wing. This photograph from the latter part of the decade shows the front of the 3646th headquarters building. In the forefront, on the left, is Col. William R. Goade, who served as the 3646th Pilot Training Wing commander from March 7, 1967, to June 2, 1969.

In August 1962, a new training device dubbed the "Suspended Agony" was rolled out at Laughlin. Laughlin was one of the first ATC Undergraduate Pilot Training (UPT) bases to include this training, which was meant to train student pilots in using and landing a parachute. This was done early on in their training so that the student pilots would know the procedures for a parachute landing if they ever had to eject from their airplane. The term itself refers to a device used for suspended harness training, pictured here in a photograph of Class 86-07. The purpose of the device is to teach student pilots the art of maneuvering the parachute with the risers. The name "Suspended Agony," a play on suspended harness training, comes from the fact that it can be quite painful to hold all of one's weight on two straps between the legs over time. Harness devices like these are also used for swing landing training, where pilots get dropped from the harness to the ground to practice parachute landing falls (or PLFs).

From July to December 1962, the Laughlin fire protection program integrated a helicopter section. Helicopters, as shown in this 1972 photograph from a fire and rescue training demonstration at Laughlin, can prove extremely helpful in transporting injured personnel or critical equipment. Today, Laughlin's fire department no longer has a helicopter section but can call on partner organizations for helicopter support and airlift if needed.

On December 7, 1962, Laughlin's first undergraduate pilot training class, Class 63-D, graduated. Of the original 23 students, only 18 were able to make it all the way through the rigorous training to graduation. This picture shows a class of undergraduate pilots at Laughlin in 1970, by which point the program was running like a well-oiled machine.

On December 10, 1962, an auxiliary runway opened at Eagle Pass, Texas, for Laughlin's use on touch-and-go landings for T-37 aircraft. This auxiliary runway would be operated until 1991, when it was finally closed down. In its place, a new auxiliary runway was opened at Spofford, Texas. The photograph here shows one of Laughlin's two on-base swimming pools, this one for the officer's club, in 1961.

Laughlin has to be able to support its student and permanent population with everything they need, including medical services. Ensuring that pilots are safe to fly is a very important job, as is caring for their general health and the health of their families. This photograph shows some of Laughlin's medical facilities in 1960.

Beginning on July 15, 1963, ATC chose Laughlin to test an experimental 10-class UPT program. It necessitated the acceleration of Classes 64-C through 64-H so the new "X" course could be phased in. This new, accelerated course comprised 45 weeks with 210 hours of flying versus the standard 55 week/262-hour syllabus. With work comes play, though. This photograph is from the 1964 Air Amistad air show at Laughlin.

In August 1963, the local flying area expanded to approximately 15,000 square miles. There is usually something of a contest for space around bases as neighboring communities expand. Laughlin has been fortunate in having a very supportive community in Del Rio, however. In this photograph from November 5, 1963, Del Rio mayor Major Dobkins presents the Texas flag to Col. August F. Taute, commander of Laughlin's 3646th Pilot Training Wing.

On October 12, 1963, the Laughlin golf course opened, pictured here a few decades later. It was called the Leaning Pine Golf Course from its construction in 1963 until December 2020, when it was renamed for the first time ever to Desert Oaks Golf Course. It was felt the new name was more fitting with the Laughlin climate.

On February 12, 1964, Laughlin Air Force Base opened a permanent runway supervisory unit to enhance safety and control of the runway for tower operators and pilots. The unit was the first of its kind in the Air Force. The winter of 1964 also saw snow at Laughlin, as shown in this photograph, a rare occurrence in southwestern Texas.

On May 28, 1964, Laughlin's first T-38A Talon arrived. It was christened the *City of Del Rio* by base leadership. These T-38s would replace the old T-33s that had been flown since the 1950s, and T-38s are still in use today—making them Laughlin Air Force Base's oldest flying aircraft. Ten years later, in 1974, a group of Laughlin pilots approach their T-38s in flight gear.

On September 24, 1964, Laughlin began assisting with local flood relief efforts after a slow-moving storm system inundated the local area with up to 10 inches of rain. On June 11, 1965, Laughlin again provided local area support, this time to victims of flooding in Sanderson, Texas, a town about two hours west of Del Rio. The picture here is from that second air rescue mission.

On February 8, 1965, Class 66-A started UPT, and the new T-38 officially entered the pilot training program. At that time, Col. Rowland O. Mosher, pictured here, was the wing commander for the 3646th. Taking the post on February 7, 1964, he would turn it over to Col. Frank M. Madsen Jr. on August 27, 1965.

On June 4, 1965, the first civilian instructor pilot checkout program began at Laughlin Air Force Base, where civilian instructors taught military pilots in the T-41 Mescalero. They flew out of the Del Rio International Airport instead of on base. Laughlin began actual instruction in the T-41 on August 9, 1965. Class 67-A became the first Laughlin class to use this airplane, pictured here in 1968.

Beginning in March 1966, Laughlin's enlisted personnel were freed from what had been called kitchen police (or KP) duties, as civilians took over the on-base kitchens. From that time forward, airmen no longer had to peel potatoes but could rely instead on talented civilian food service workers to provide them with world-quality meals.

Following initial tests at Laughlin Air Force Base on March 22, 1966, parasailing was made part of the training program at all undergraduate navigator and pilot training bases across ATC. It would remain a part of training until October 1, 2007, when it was removed—making Class 09-01 the first class not to undergo parasail training in over 40 years. This picture is from one of the earliest parasailing classes in 1966.

The Wing Operations Division devised and initiated the continuous flow aircraft launch concept to smooth out air traffic operations. Planes would launch every three minutes, eliminating the "busy" and "lull" periods that marked flight operations before. This new program was put into effect beginning on July 8, 1966. This photograph captured Laughlin's main entrance gate in 1967, as the base continued to thrive.

On Saturday, December 3, 1966, Pres. Lyndon B. Johnson visited Laughlin Air Force Base, in Del Rio, and Ciudad Acuña, Mexico, to discuss the progress of the Amistad Dam with Mexican president Gustavo Díaz Ordaz. This picture was from his ride through town with the Mexican president (standing in vehicle at right). President Johnson was accompanied on this trip by his wife, the secretary of state, and the Mexican ambassador.

The next presidential visit was on September 8, 1969, when Pres. Richard M. Nixon visited Laughlin to dedicate the Amistad Dam in Del Rio with Mexican president Gustavo Díaz Ordaz. Both men are pictured here embracing before the completed dam, continuing the abrazo tradition first started in 1960 by Pres. Dwight D. Eisenhower and Pres. López Mateos with the signing of the treaty to build the dam.

In 1970, Laughlin itself hosted friends from Mexico. Here, Lt. Gen. George B. Simler (second from left), ATC commander, shakes hands with Glen Garrett (right), executive director of the Texas Good Neighbor Committee. Pictured with Simler and Garrett are, from left to right, Jesus Maria Ramon, former mayor of Acuña, Mexico; Col. Donald J. Ferris, 3646th Pilot Training Wing commander; and Raul Gonzalez, president of Acuña's Good Neighbor Committee.

In 1970, Chief Master Sergeant Thomas N. Barnes became Laughlin's first senior airman advisor. This position later became the senior enlisted advisor and today is called the command chief master sergeant. He was Laughlin's very first due to the fact that the position itself was just getting started. He would go on from Laughlin to Air Training Command, where he was its second senior enlisted advisor, and from there, he would become the fourth chief master sergeant of the Air Force and the first African American chief master sergeant of the Air Force. In 2010, he was remembered at Laughlin when, as shown in this picture, a street was dedicated in his name. From left to right are Maj. Gen. Alfred Stewart, Air Force Personnel Center commander; Theresa Neal, Hazel Lamb, and Thyra Barnes, all daughters of Chief Master Sergeant Barnes; Col. Tom Murphy, 47th Flying Training Wing commander; and Thyra Barnes's unidentified guest.

Five

The 47th Flying Training Wing 1972–1994

On September 1, 1972, the 3646th Pilot Training Wing was inactivated and the 47th Flying Training Wing (47 FTW) was activated to maintain the heritage of the 47th Bombardment Wing.

The 47th Bombardment Wing, Light (47 BW), was established on July 28, 1947, and organized at Biggs Field, Texas, on August 15, 1947. Utilizing a number of World War II squadrons that specialized in night flying (many of whose descendant units still serve the 47 FTW today), the 47 BW's role in the years between 1947 and 1949 was to train and provide instruction on night tactical operations, to conduct firepower demonstrations, and to participate in tactical exercises. On November 19, 1948, the wing moved to Barksdale Air Force Base, Louisiana, where it became the first wing in the Air Force to receive the North American B-45A Tornado—America's first operational jet bomber. A number of complications made it difficult for the wing to become operational in this period, and due to budgetary constraints within the Department of the Air Force (and the Department of Defense as a whole), the Air Force inactivated the 47 BW entirely on October 2, 1949.

The next time the 47 BW was revived was on March 12, 1951, under Tactical Air Command at Langley Air Force Base in Virginia. Its mission was again primarily to fly the B-45. Crews became proficient with special weapon delivery but also provided combat crew training in the B-26. They additionally operated the US Air Force Air Crew School (Light Bombardment and Tactical Reconnaissance, Night Photographic). They were soon positioned in Sculthorpe, England (June 1, 1952), with select squadrons at times operating from Royal Air Force Alconbury. During the wing's latter years as a bombardment wing, it was redesignated the 47th Bombardment Wing, Tactical (1955), and briefly conducted aerial refueling with the Boeing KB-50J Superfortress (1960–1962) before being inactivated on June 22, 1962.

The 47th was revived again a decade later on September 1, 1972, this time as the 47th Flying Training Wing, and was instructed to take over the undergraduate pilot training mission at Laughlin Air Force Base. The 47 FTW continues to fly at Laughlin today.

On September 1, 1972, the 47th Flying Training Wing was activated at Laughlin Air Force Base. The base at the time looked much as it does in this 1971 photograph. From this angle, one can see the airfield with planes, the control tower, several administrative buildings and dormitories, and a number of key operations and maintenance facilities as they were arranged at the time. Much has changed in the decades since this photograph was taken, but the base's basic footprint remains the same, just as it has since 1942. One thing that is notable about the 47th Flying Training Wing, however—in addition to its lineage as the 47th Bombardment Wing—is the fact that it has served as Laughlin Air Force Base's host unit longer than any other unit (by far). From 1972 to the present day, nearly 50 years at the time of this book's publication, the 47 FTW has called Laughlin Air Force Base its home.

The 47 FTW for the most part simply took over for the 3646th Pilot Training Wing, also being charged with undergraduate pilot training. In fact, the last commander of the 3646th and the first commander of the 47th were the same man, Col. Charles E. Woods, pictured here. Class 73-03, already in training when the 47th replaced the 3646th, became the 47 FTW's first graduating class on September 22, 1972.

Starting on July 21, 1975, Air Training Command (ATC) directed the 47 FTW to implement the Security Assistance Training Program (SATP) syllabus, which increased foreign student training by having them go through regular UPT. After the SATP was adopted, Chile, Iran, Nicaragua, and Saudi Arabia began sending pilot trainees through Laughlin Air Force Base. This image shows a diverse team of Laughlin personnel working on a T-38A in 1972.

On September 16, 1972, shortly after the 47 FTW was activated, the secretary of the Air Force named Laughlin as a base that was once more potentially facing closure. On March 30, 1977, the secretary of the Air Force instead closed Webb Air Force Base in Texas and Craig Air Force Base in Alabama, sparing Laughlin. In this photograph from 1977, Laughlin tower crew operate out of the air traffic control tower.

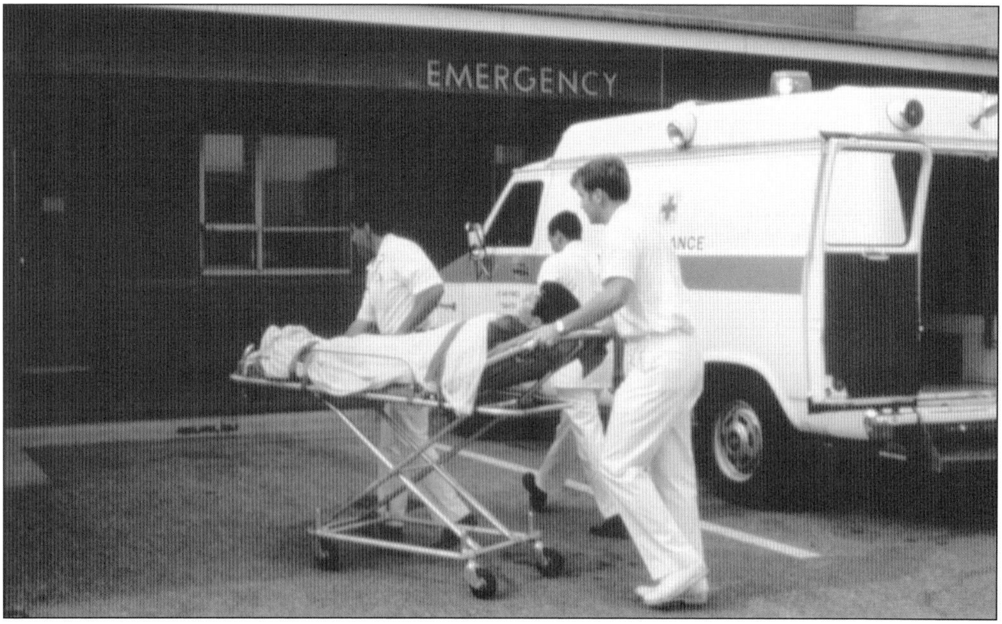

Also in 1977, hospital personnel moved into their new facility on base. The move took place on October 19, 1977, and the formal dedication of the new hospital was on December 1, 1977. This photograph features 47th Medical Group first responders practicing patient transport during a 1978 exercise at the new facility.

On April 23, 1978, the 47th Security Police Division was notified that it was chosen as the best in the Air Force for that year. This photograph of a security police officer at Laughlin's west gate is also from 1978. The 47th Security Police Division would eventually be organized into a squadron and then become what it is known as today, the 47th Security Forces Squadron, in 1997.

Section I of the new flight simulator building was completed on November 22, 1978, and was accepted by the Air Force. In April 1979, the wing received updated simulators, which allowed students to practice instrument flying. This saw a reduction in overall flight hours as simulator training increased. This photograph from 1979 shows a student pilot learning on one of the T-37 simulators.

On November 28, 1979, Iranian students at Laughlin were placed on "ineffective" status due to the Iran hostage crisis. Wing personnel continued training members from Italy, Kenya, Nigeria, Saudi Arabia, and Zaire. On April 10, 1980, all Iranian students and dependents departed Laughlin Air Force Base for Houston, Texas, from where they would return to Iran. This photograph is of Laughlin's airfield in 1972, and the aircraft pictured are T-37s.

Maj. Gen. Charles F. Cleveland, ATC vice commander (and a former 47 FTW commander), unveiled a bronze plaque dedicating the new instrument flight simulator building in memory of Chief Master Sergeant Daniel P. Jarvis, pictured here, on December 13, 1979. Chief Jarvis had been Laughlin Air Force Base's superintendent of training devices from June 23, 1971, to shortly before his death in 1977. The Jarvis Building still houses the wing's flight simulators today.

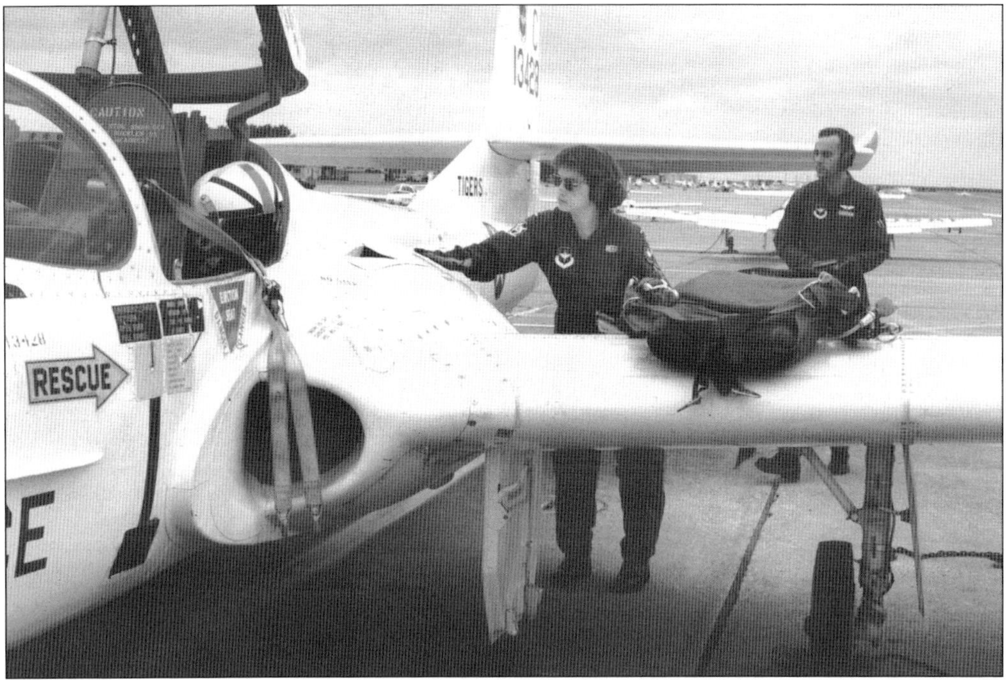

Laughlin's first female instructor pilot (IP), 2nd Lt. Cyndhi Hughes, reported for duty at the 85th Flying Training Squadron on July 5, 1980. Soon, Laughlin and the rest of the Air Force were finding that female leaders were indeed a huge boon to the organization and the nation itself, as in the case of Second Lieutenant Reed, pictured here inspecting her aircraft in 1982.

On February 25, 1981, 2nd Lt. Kimberly Baird became the 47th Flying Training Wing's first female graduate when she graduated with 46 others as part of Class 81-03. She is pictured here preparing for a training sortie prior to her graduation. The US Air Force only began to allow women to train as pilots in 1976.

Laughlin's new recreation area at Lake Amistad was officially opened on May 2, 1981. This allowed personnel at Laughlin to take advantage of the beautiful Amistad reservoir, created with the completion of the Amistad Dam in 1969. And later in the 1980s, the wing would shift from a military maintenance squadron (pictured here at work) to a civilian directorate.

On July 2, 1982, the base celebrated Laughlin's 40th anniversary. From this 40th anniversary, Laughlin's personnel began identifying themselves as "Team XL," thanks to a logo generated by John Stein out of public affairs. XL are the Roman numerals for 40 and, of course, also sound like "excel." It caught on fast and stuck, as evidenced in this photograph from 1988 at the headquarters of the 86th Flying Training Squadron.

On August 1, 1983, the 47th Flying Training Wing took a giant step forward in automation when it received 11 brand-new word processors. Laughlin was entering the computer age, slowly but surely, with the rest of the world. Here, the 2108th Information Systems Squadron, forerunners of today's 47th Communications Squadron, is hard at work on the new technology in 1987.

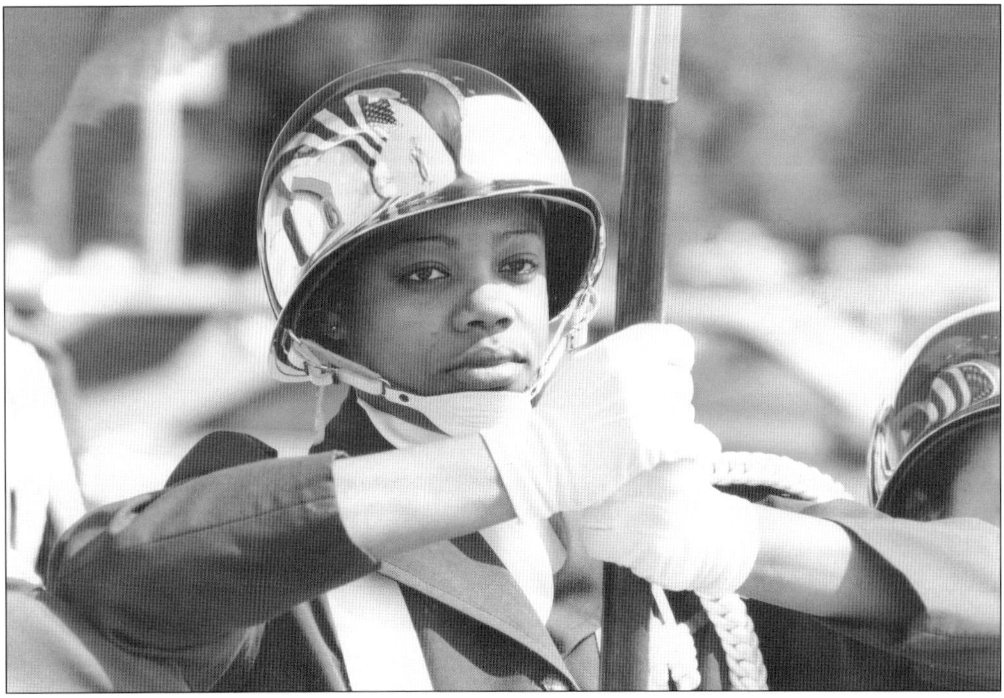

From August 1 to August 6, 1983, members of Tisch-Avnet Producers shot portions of what would become the 1984–1985 television series *Call to Glory* at Laughlin. And on October 14, 1983, an NBC production crew spent the day at Laughlin filming the final episode of a five-part series on what the Air Force considered the "Right Stuff." Photographed here is A1C Carlene Thomas, Laughlin Air Force Base Honor Guard, in 1987.

On January 27, 1984, Laughlin maintainers received a fully operational centralized aircraft support system, which provided electrical power and air supply for aircraft starts and troubleshooting, reducing their reliance on certain pieces of aerospace ground equipment. A couple of years later, Laughlin's maintenance squadron was ranked number one in the Air Force, as shown in this photograph with S.M.Sgt. Bill Wilmot (left, the squadron's first sergeant) and Maj. John D. Whitfield (right).

The "Avenue of Flags" opened in front of the wing headquarters building on May 1, 1984. Until the new wing headquarters building was constructed a couple of decades later, this display was used regularly; it is pictured here at a special 1984 retreat ceremony. There was room for up to 100 flags if the occasion called for it.

Dedication ceremonies were held for the new enlisted dormitory, Ricks Hall, on June 15, 1984. Wing leadership named the new building, pictured here, to honor the memory of Phillip A. Ricks, one of Laughlin's most devoted supporters in the Del Rio community. Currently, this building is not being used, but wing leadership hopes to renovate it and reopen it soon for dormitory use.

On June 2, 1988, the Airport Radar Service Area was implemented at Laughlin. The Federal Aviation Administration (FAA) required all pilots, military and civilian, to maintain two-way radio communications with Laughlin Air Traffic Control in order to resolve potential conflicts between instrument flight rule and visual flight rule traffic. Pictured here are tower personnel hard at work in 1988.

On November 8, 1988, the 47th Flying Training Wing received notification that its aircraft maintenance function would convert from a military to a civil service operation. This was due to the fact that it was determined that civil service provided the most efficient organization (MEO) for this function, following an earlier study demonstrating as much, and implementation began in February 1989. The conversion was completed on August 20, 1989, with aircraft maintenance at Laughlin Air Force Base becoming a completely civilian-manned operation on that date. Laughlin's maintenance team remains a civil service directorate today, hiring the majority of its technicians and maintainers from the local community—and from Del Rio, Texas, in particular. This photograph from July 1989 shows S.Sgt. Carl Roberts (kneeling), 47th Organizational Maintenance Squadron crew chief, demonstrating T-38A engine run-up procedures for Robert Marquez, a new civil service crew chief.

In April 1989, Congress designated Laughlin Air Force Base a remote facility for morale, welfare, and recreation (MWR)—making it the only facility so designated in Air Training Command. This allowed for more appropriated fund support for MWR activities, helping the base provide more entertainment to wing personnel. Del Rio, Texas, is considered somewhat off the beaten path and far from the big cities. Even so, remoteness aside, the city and the base still know how to have a good time. Pictured here is a poster advertising a 1986 air show as the "best event of the year," with semiregular air shows like this one being one of the ways Laughlin and Del Rio enjoy fun in the sun together. These air shows were called Air Amistad for decades, though more recently they have been known under other names, such as the Fiesta of Flight exposition in 2018. (Courtesy of the James L. Long Collection at the Laughlin Heritage Foundation.)

On May 26, 1989, the Ribas-Dominicci Plaza was named in honor of Maj. Fernando Ribas-Dominicci. Major Ribas-Dominicci, an F-111 Aardvark pilot killed in the April 1986 raid on Libya (Operation El Dorado Canyon), graduated from Laughlin Air Force Base with Class 77-05. This photograph from 2020 captures the memorial to Major Ribas-Dominicci, which the Laughlin Heritage Foundation helped to raise funds for. It still stands in Ribas-Dominicci Plaza today.

The 47th Civil Engineer Squadron's Prime BEEF team departed for Charleston, South Carolina, on February 27, 1990, to help the city following Hurricane Hugo. Prime BEEF stands for Prime Base Engineer Emergency Force, and one thing these quick-reaction teams can do is respond to major disasters. This photograph, depicting 47th Civil Engineering Squadron commander Lt. Col. Bill Norton (standing at left) and team members, is from a May 1987 deployment.

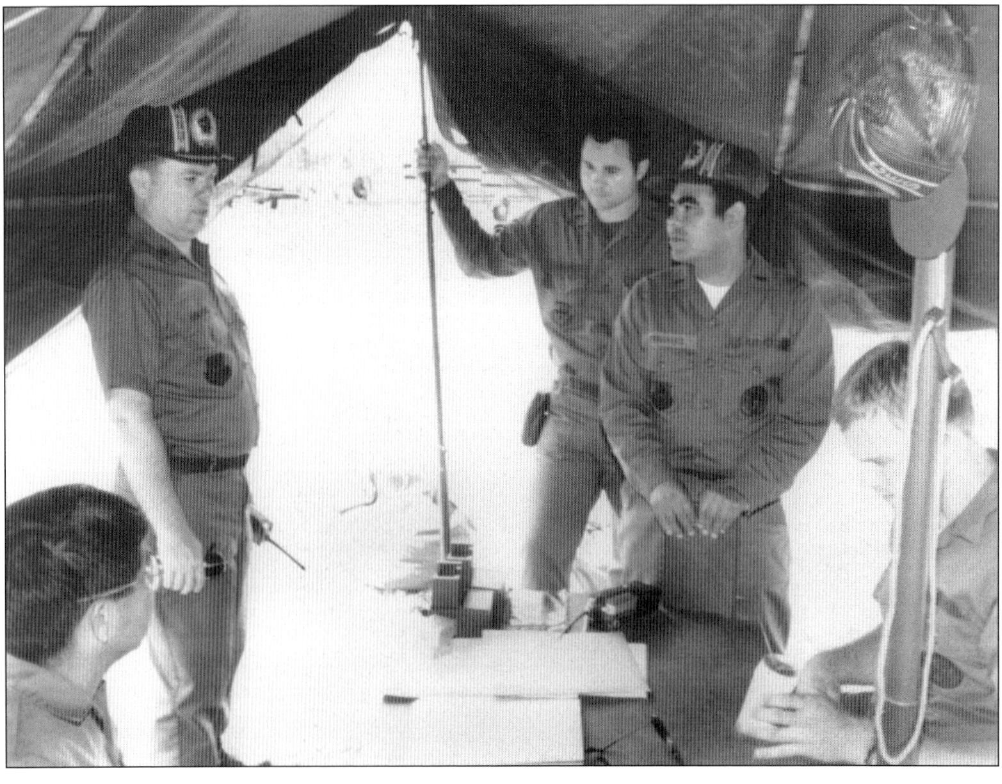

To prepare for specialized undergraduate pilot training, a new way to train students, ATC activated three squadrons at Laughlin on April 2, 1990: the 39th, 84th, and 87th Flying Training Squadrons. The 39th was a forerunner to the present-day Operations Support Squadron, and its activation led to the inactivation of the 47th Student Squadron (with the 39th taking over the mission). This 1982 photograph shows academic classroom training.

On April 9, 1990, the wing established a vocational education program with Del Rio dubbed the Grow Your Own program, which taught basic aircraft maintenance at the local high school. This photograph from April 1993 shows Robert Sandoval (front left) and Wesley Jackson (front right) of Laughlin Civil Service Aircraft Maintenance accepting the Daedalian Trophy. ATC commander Gen. Henry Viccellio Jr. (back left) and 47 FTW commander Col. Kenneth W. Hess (back right) are behind.

As part of organizational changes throughout the Air Force, the wing gained control of the 2108th Communications Squadron on October 1, 1990. USAF Hospital Laughlin was redesignated the 47 FTW Hospital at that same time. The 2108th Communications Squadron would eventually become the 47th Communications Squadron on July 1, 1994. The squadron was also called "the Scorpions" due to its squadron emblem, pictured here on the wall of its building.

A new auxiliary field at Spofford, Texas, pictured here in 1997, opened for touch-and-go landing operations on January 28, 1991. As a result, the wing canceled its lease on the field at Eagle Pass. There were multiple reasons for the move to Spofford, but mostly it had to do with minimizing safety risks.

On May 16, 1991, Class 91-09 became the first group eligible for "banked assignments." Due to the end of the Cold War, pilot production at that time outpaced pilot need because of an expected reduction of Air Force operational end strengths. This photograph from 1987 shows Amn. Vincent Garr of 47 FTW Life Support (standing) fitting a helmet for a student pilot at Laughlin.

A huge change took place on December 16, 1991: Wing organization changed from a tri-deputy system to the objective wing concept. The end result of the reorganization was that there was a single wing commander with a single vice commander and no deputy commanders. Instead, the wing was organized into groups, with group commanders reporting directly to the wing commander. Pictured here is Laughlin's main gate in 1989.

On September 1, 1992, ATC ordered the 84th and 85th Flying Training Squadrons (flying the T-37) and the 86th and 87th Flying Training Squadrons (flying the T-38) to merge. The 84th and 86th inactivated. This photograph from 1987 shows Sergeant Justus (left) of the Aerospace Physiology Lab giving a thumbs up to a student pilot who had successfully completed the checklist for a physiological emergency during ground training.

On November 18, 1993, Laughlin's first SUPT class, 95-02, started. This photograph shows students at work during the academic portion of their three-phase SUPT training. Phase I is academics. Phase II is where students learn how to fly on the basic trainer aircraft (today the T-6, but at this time the T-37). After Phase II, students specialize into the type of aircraft they will be piloting (bomber/fighter, airlift/tanker, or helicopter).

On November 19, 1993, the 47 FTW received its first T-1A aircraft, tail number 92-0342, which would be the plane utilized in SUPT by pilots flying the airlift/tanker track. Specialized undergraduate pilot training is still used today. On December 1, 1993, the 86 Flying Training Squadron was activated once more and was given the responsibility of training pilots on the new T-1A, pictured here in a photograph from 1994.

During the transition to SUPT, the 47th Flying Training Wing was commanded by Brig. Gen. Kenneth W. Hess, pictured here. It was the only time the 47 FTW has been commanded by a general at Laughlin Air Force Base, which goes to demonstrate just how important this transition in training was for the Air Force.

d Lt Mark Forkner (left), student, and
:apt Perry Peter, flight commander, check
ut the T-1A before taking the first
raining flight on 6 June 1994. Not
ictured: Student Capt Keith Gailey

(USAF Photo Jun 94)

The first SUPT class, Class 95-02, entered Phase III training on May 24, 1994. Four students went to the fighter/bomber track, and 17 (including Air National Guard and Air Force Reserve students) entered the airlift/tanker track. On June 6, 1994, Capt. Keith Gailey and 2nd Lt. Mark Forkner of Class 95-02 made the first student sortie in the T-1A Jayhawk. Capt. Perry Peter was the instructor pilot (IP) with the 86th Flying Training Squadron. Since its reactivation in late 1993, the 86th Flying Training Squadron (86 FTS) has continued to teach the T-1A aircraft. The T-1 is the largest airplane in the 47th Flying Training Wing's fleet, and this medium-range, twin-engine jet trainer is used at Laughlin to train those who enter the airlift/tanker track. At other locations, including the Navy and Marine Corps, it is also used to support navigator training.

In September 1994, Maj. Mark A. Kyle became the first pilot to graduate from the T-1A program at Laughlin. Kyle, a rated reserve pilot with 2,800 hours in the H-3 and H-60 helicopters, also flew the C-130 and eventually became commander of the 22nd Air Force. This photograph from 1994 shows the inside of a T-1A cockpit.

On September 28, 1994, Laughlin's last traditional undergraduate pilot training (UPT) class, Class 94-15, graduated. It was composed of 20 students, four of whom were Turkish Air Force pilots. This photograph from 1990 depicts 87th Flying Training Squadron (87 FTS) instructor pilot Capt. Todd Miller (center) discussing the T-38A Talon with a student pilot and a civilian maintenance technician.

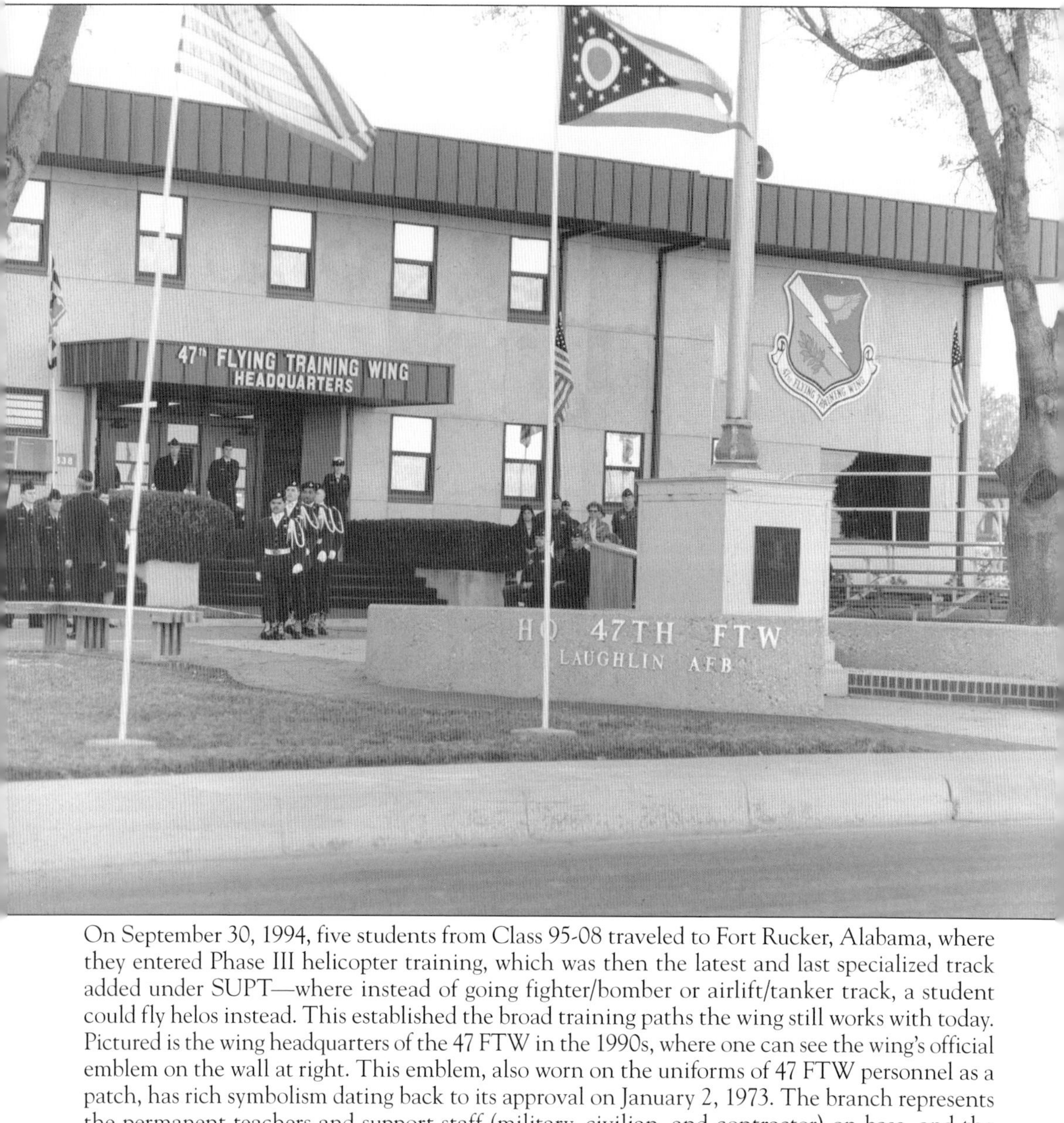

On September 30, 1994, five students from Class 95-08 traveled to Fort Rucker, Alabama, where they entered Phase III helicopter training, which was then the latest and last specialized track added under SUPT—where instead of going fighter/bomber or airlift/tanker track, a student could fly helos instead. This established the broad training paths the wing still works with today. Pictured is the wing headquarters of the 47 FTW in the 1990s, where one can see the wing's official emblem on the wall at right. This emblem, also worn on the uniforms of 47 FTW personnel as a patch, has rich symbolism dating back to its approval on January 2, 1973. The branch represents the permanent teachers and support staff (military, civilian, and contractor) on base, and the wing represents the students—past, present, and future—who the 47 FTW teaches to fly. The lightning bolt represents the wing's expeditionary taskings, whereby the wing deploys personnel to support the US military at large.

Six

Laughlin Today and Laughlin Tomorrow 1994–2020

The establishment of the objective wing base layout and the introduction of specialized undergraduate pilot training represented significant changes in the way the US Air Force organized its bases and trained its student pilots. Naturally, then, these both resulted in tremendous changes at Laughlin Air Force Base as well. In addition to these two major shake-ups, the past 30 years have seen a number of other historically important events and transformations in the way the base operates, with many more changes likely ahead as new, emerging technologies like virtual reality and artificial intelligence alter the way the Air Force looks at training and the way the world looks at air power. This chapter is dedicated to bringing the history of Laughlin to its latest conclusion.

By the mid-1990s, following the collapse of the Soviet Union and the conclusion of the Gulf War, the Air Force saw that the world was changing, and it needed to change with it in order to maintain its competitive edge in the new styles of warfare that were emerging. This also included, of course, responding to congressional budget and manning cuts as a result of the collapse of the rival superpower against which the United States had spent the last half-century posturing itself.

At Laughlin Air Force Base, the wing and base's response to these changes were predominately captured in the worn-and-torn phrases "do more with less" and "flexibility is the key to air power." But truly, it was just a matter of adapting to the changing requirements of the nation, and the 47th Flying Training Wing rose to the occasion, becoming in these years the premier, number-one producer of US Air Force pilots. This chapter examines these transformations, the setbacks and obstacles that stood in the way of achieving this success, and how the wing and the base have overcome them through adaptability, creativity, and the sheer dedication of the airmen who have served and who continue to serve at Laughlin Air Force Base.

On February 3, 1995, the 47th Medical Group used one of the new Laughlin T-1s in a medical evacuation for the first time. Faced with an emergency neonatal case that could not be handled locally, medical personnel had to quickly transport the patient to San Antonio. Flight surgeon Capt. Greg Gardner had designed a prototype stretcher for use on a T-1, and, thanks to that, both mother and baby survived.

The last class of banked airlift/tanker pilots entered training at Laughlin on June 12, 1996. A total of 305 banked pilots had trained since September 1994. Pictured in this 1995 photograph, from left to right, Captain Finnegan, Captain Pogorin, and Captain Faidley, three airlift/tanker pilots in the 86th Flying Training Squadron at Laughlin, are reviewing documentation.

The 47th Dental Squadron was inactivated on June 13, 1997. It became a dental flight within the 47th Medical Operations Squadron (47 MDOS) instead. This photograph from 2001 shows a member of the 47 MDOS at work. In 2019, the 47 MDOS was replaced with the 47th Operational Medical Readiness Squadron as a result of legislative changes that centralized all of the branch military medical groups under the Defense Health Agency.

On July 1, 1997, Air Education and Training Command (or AETC, as ATC was renamed) redesignated the 47th Security Police Squadron to the 47th Security Forces Squadron, which Laughlin's patrolling and security forces remain known as today. The Laughlin airman in this photograph from 2006 guards visiting F-22 Raptors from the 325th Fighter Wing.

In April 1998, effective with Class 99-01, AETC moved training for bomber track students to the T-1A. This would not last long, with bomber track pilots eventually moving back to the T-38s in April 2000, starting with Class 01-01. In this 1994 photograph, a T-1A is on display. Note the "XL" on the tail. This is an identifier of all Laughlin airplanes.

On April 1, 1998, the 96th Flying Training Squadron (96 FTS), an Air Force Reserve squadron, was activated to provide instructor pilot augmentation to the wing as a classic associate unit. The 96 FTS still supports pilot training at Laughlin. This 2013 photograph shows Maj. Kristie Hayward—who was named the 340th Flying Training Group's support officer of the year for 2012—standing beside the 96 FTS's emblem.

Capt. Phillip "Slim" Thompson and his student, 2nd Lt. Mary J. Harris of Class 99-03, flew the 85th Flying Training Squadron's one millionth T-37 hour on May 8, 1998. This picture from 2002 shows four T-37s in a flying formation over Del Rio, Texas, near Lake Amistad. The T-37 was the airplane that students first learned how to fly in these days before tracking into the T-1 or T-38.

On August 23, 1998, a devastating flood was caused by the remnants of Tropical Storm Charley, which dumped over 10 inches of rain on Laughlin proper and almost 19 inches of rain on downtown Del Rio. The flooding set the training timeline behind until February 24, 1999. This photograph shows some of the damage that was wrought, flooding the ramp and the runways as well as most of the base.

On December 14, 1998, a Laughlin T-37, tail number 57-2318, achieved a major milestone when it surpassed 20,000 hours of flight time in a ceremonial flight marking the occasion. Lt. Col. Jason Barlow, 85 FTS commander, and Lt. Col. Kevin Keith, 84 FTS commander, flew the sortie. In this photograph from 2002, a T-37 comes in for a landing.

On April 21, 1999, the 47 FTW and the San Felipe Del Rio Consolidated Independent School District revalidated the formal Grow Your Own training program, where local students were trained in aircraft maintenance in preparation for a job in the field following graduation. This established the program into its 10th year. Here, Laughlin maintenance personnel of various experience levels work in the tire shop in 2002.

In October 1999, in addition to its existing role overseeing enlisted controller training, the 47th Operations Support Squadron (47 OSS) gained responsibility for officer training under the Officer Training Program (OTP). In this 1999 picture, 47 OSS personnel work in Laughlin's RAPCON, or Radar Approach Control, section to help manage and direct aircraft safely.

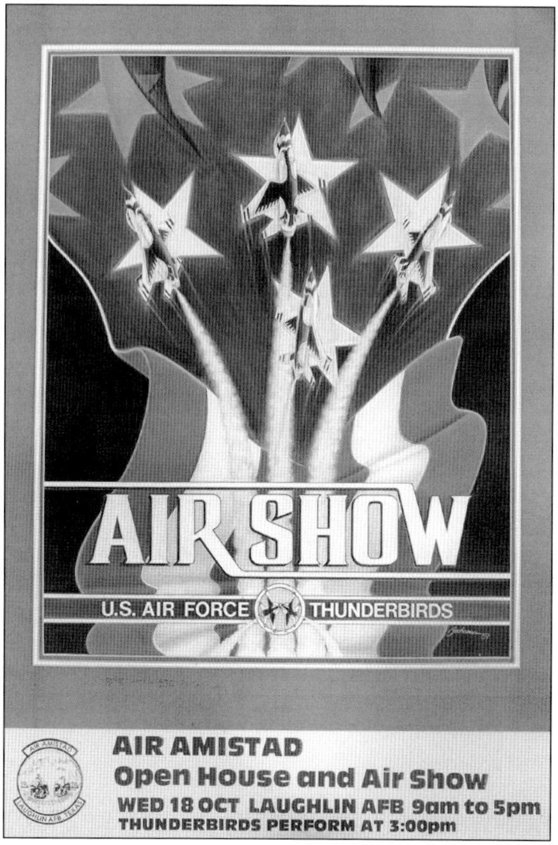

In April 2000, the 47 FTW implemented the First Term Airman Center (FTAC) as directed by the Air Force and AETC. The FTAC was designed to help first duty station airmen transition from a training-only environment to a mission-oriented one. This year also saw the first air show of the new millennium at Laughlin, advertised here. (Courtesy of the James L. Long Collection at the Laughlin Heritage Foundation.)

In March 2001, AETC changed Laughlin's aircraft maintenance status from a most efficient organization (MEO) to a regular aircraft maintenance organization. Here, a Laughlin maintenance technician is pictured working on one of the 47 FTW's T-38 Talons in 2004. In the background, one can see parts of the rest of the T-38 fleet as well as a number of maintenance and operations buildings.

Pictured here in an official Air Force portrait, Col. Eric J. Rosborg, the 47th Flying Training Wing's commander at the time, hosted Laughlin Air Force Base's first Aerospace Power Call on October 12, 2001. Brig. Gen. Robin Olds, USAF (Ret.), a triple ace and aviation legend, was the guest speaker. The base has hosted many distinguished military and civilian guests over the years.

On October 26, 2001, wing leaders dedicated the Operations Training Complex (OTC) in honor of Maj. Rudolf Anderson Jr., a former Laughlin U-2 pilot shot down and killed during the Cuban Missile Crisis. His daughter and one of his two sons attended the ceremony. They are pictured here with family and Colonel Rosborg, the wing commander.

Three 87 FTS instructor pilots (IPs) created a break-in-training syllabus for students facing excessive times between SUPT graduation and Introduction to Fighter Fundamentals (IFF). The new program was released on March 6, 2002, and AETC implemented it command-wide as the T-38 Graduate Aviation Program. In this photograph from 2000, an 87 FTS IP works with three student pilots during a brief.

On March 8, 2002, to honor the victims of the September 11, 2001, terrorist attacks on the United States, wing personnel unveiled the "Let's Roll" nose art on an 87 FTS T-38A Talon. Pictured here in 2003 are, from left to right, Gen. Donald G. Cook, his wife, and 47 FTW commander Col. Daniel P. Woodward during a visit to the base by General Cook, who was then the AETC commander.

A severe hailstorm struck Laughlin on April 7, 2002. Even though maintenance had taken the necessary aircraft sheltering actions earlier that day, more than half of the base's T-37s received enough damage to render them unflyable. Laughlin weather is often unpredictable, as in a 2007 snowstorm, after which the fire department had to deice the wing headquarters building (pictured here) to prevent ice from falling on and injuring people.

On April 8, 2002, Col. Eric J. Rosborg installed 21 Del Rio civic leaders as honorary commanders. He hoped the Honorary Commander Program would further strengthen the strong bonds between the base and Del Rio, and it has continued into the present day. This photograph from 2003 shows wing commander Col. Daniel P. Woodward continuing the tradition by naming Del Rio mayor Dora G. Alcalá the wing's honorary commander.

On July 8, 2002, the wing shipped out a T-37B (tail number 58-1956) to the Aircraft Maintenance and Regeneration Center (AMARC) at Davis-Monthan Air Force Base. This started the wing's T-37B drawdown as it began preparations for conversion to the T-6A Texan II. This photograph shows the base footprint in 1997, during the heyday of the T-37B Tweet at Laughlin.

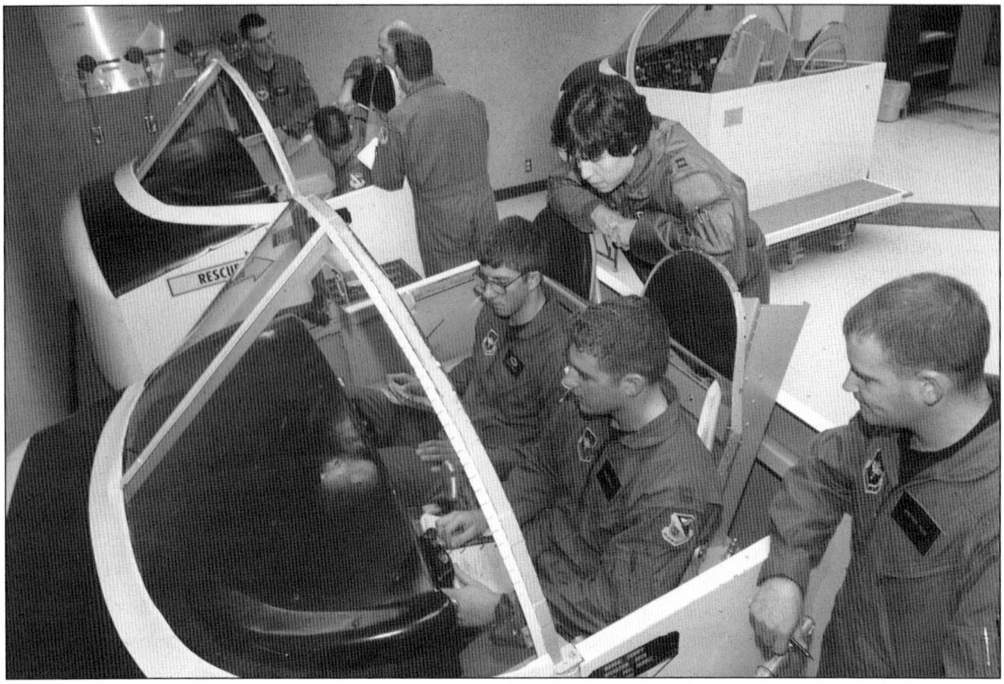

The 47th Flying Training Wing received certification on initial T-6A operational flight and instrument flight trainers on August 5, 2002. Additionally, it also received certification on unit training devices. These would eventually replace the T-37B trainers, pictured here in 2003, in use by student pilots.

On August 9, 2002, as part of an Air Force directive, aircraft maintenance moved from operations to maintenance groups Air Force–wide. Locally, aircraft maintenance moved to the wing staff as a directorate, since as a civilian-led organization, it could not be a military group. In this photograph from 2004, maintenance personnel help guide a T-38 Talon into a hangar.

On November 15, 2002, Laughlin Air Force Base officially received its first T-6A Texan II. This aircraft would eventually replace the T-37B Tweet as the primary trainer (that is, the plane that students first learn how to fly on) at Laughlin. In this photograph from 2004, a T-6 (with a front propeller) and T-37 fly together.

When flight training resumed on January 6, 2003, after a holiday break, air traffic and radar approach controllers (RAPCON) began to work out of their combined facility in the new operations building. Previously the two had been separated, with the tower standing alone and RAPCON, pictured here in 1997, in its own building.

Class 04-04, the first 47 FTW class with students identified to train in the T-6A, entered training on January 8, 2003. At the time, some of the students still used the T-37, as not enough T-6s were available for all. Here, a maintenance technician and pilots can be seen with a number of T-37s in 2001.

Beginning on February 10, 2003, AETC transferred the Air Traffic Controller OTP to Moody Air Force Base in Georgia. This took away some of the 47 OSS's burden concerning upgrade training, as tower/radar approach controller three-level manning remained above US Air Force and AETC averages. This photograph from 2002 shows operators working inside the control tower.

On February 21, 2003, 2nd Lt. Donald Hicks, a student pilot in Class 04-04, and his IP, Capt. Darrell F. Judy—84 FTS K flight commander—flew the first T-6A Texan II training sortie conducted by the 47th Flying Training Wing. Here, two pilots prepare for a T-6 sortie in 2003.

On March 21, 2003, a month after the first T-6 flight by Lt. Donald Hicks and Capt. Darrell Judy, 2nd Lt. Sonny D. Baxter and 2nd Lt. Robert E. West of the 84 FTS became the wing's first students to solo in the T-6A. Later, in September, Class 04-14 became the wing's first full T-6A class. Anderson Hall, dedicated in 2001 and pictured here in 2006, is where students prepare for their flights.

On October 17, 2003, during the wing's first Pilot for a Day program, Juan Jose Morin Jr. toured Laughlin with Capt. Brad Brumbaugh, an 87 FTS IP. The Pilot for a Day program affords children with chronic disabilities or terminal illnesses a day filled with fun. This 2018 photograph of the wing's annual Junior Deployment is another kids-focused event, where military children are introduced to the (abbreviated) deployment process their parents go through.

On February 18, 2004, AETC leaders announced that they had received an infusion of funds to speed up the T-38C Propulsion Modernization Program (PMP). This meant that the 87 FTS would gain its PMP T-38Cs three years earlier than planned. This was the first major upgrade to the T-38 since it was rolled out in the 1960s. In this 1995 photograph, one of the pre-upgrade T-38s is being refueled.

On September 7, 2004, while the Tweet phaseout continued, the introduction of the T-38C also took another step forward when Maj. Ron Price, 96 FTS, and Maj. Douglas Jenkins, 87 FTS, conducted the first T-38C sortie—flying a low-level route over Big Bend National Park. This photograph shows inside the cockpit of one of the upgraded T-38Cs.

On November 19, 2004, a day after the official T-37B retirement ceremony, 2nd Lt. David Kluttz, Class 05-10, and his IP, 1st Lt. Samuel A. Moore (the final 47 FTW T-37B first assignment instructor pilot, or FAIP), became the last two pilots to fly a T-37B training sortie for the 47 FTW. Class 05-10, pictured here in front of a T-37, was the last class to train in this airplane.

Seven students from Class 05-10 also became the wing's first students to train in the T-38C, starting on November 22, 2004. Meanwhile, this photograph from September 7, 2004, captures the celebration following the last T-37B solo flight with Class 05-10. The very last student to do an initial solo flight on the outgoing T-37B, pictured here about to be thrown into the tank, was 2nd Lt. Christian Hamilton.

On December 1, 2004, the distinctive "screech" sound of flying T-37B Tweets stopped. After over 43 years, 1 million sorties, 1.5 million hours, and 12,500 students from over 40 countries, T-37B operations came to a complete halt at Laughlin when Maj. Lon Schmidt and Maj. Jorge Nuñez flew the last two XL Tweets to Davis-Monthan Air Force Base. This photograph from 1993 shows the profile of a T-37B flying off into the sunset.

On May 20, 2005, Department of Defense officials released the 2005 Base Realignment and Closure (BRAC) recommendations, and Laughlin Air Force Base survived again! Team XL gained 29 aircraft (16 T-6As and 13 T-38Cs), 162 full-time and 7 reserve personnel, and related equipment from places that closed. Further, Laughlin Air Force Base's SUPT Phase II and Introduction to Fighter Fundamentals (IFF) missions increased. Here, Laughlin students are in physiology training in 2007.

From June 19 to July 24, 2005, seven IPs from the 86 FTS, accompanied by two civilian maintainers, flew their T-1A Jayhawks to McChord Air Force Base, Washington, and took part in Air Mobility Command's Air Mobility Rodeo. The IPs flew weather-ship duties and participated in the Operational Support Airlift/Special Air Mission category. This was the first time any T-1A crews participated in the rodeo. Here, in 2004, civilian maintainers work on a T-1.

Class 05-13 graduated from pilot training on August 12, 2005, becoming the last to train in the T-38A. The wing's final T-38A, tail number 62-9654, departed Laughlin for the modification line at Randolph Air Force Base on September 2, 2005. This 2005 photograph shows a formation flight with the last T-38A model over Lake Amistad.

On December 15, 2006, after nearly 55 years of publication, the *Border Eagle*, Laughlin's official newspaper, ceased publication. The *Del Rio News Herald* continued to publish the *Laughlin Herald*, however, until the *Del Rio News Herald* itself became an economic casualty of the COVID-19 pandemic in 2020, closing its offices. Also in 2006, the new (and current) base headquarters building was dedicated in the ceremony pictured here.

The 434th Fighter Training Squadron formally activated and came under the control of the 47th Operations Group on July 19, 2007. This squadron initially conducted Introduction to Fighter Fundamentals (IFF) training at Laughlin, instructing recent specialized undergraduate pilot training graduates who were bound for fighter planes. Here, a 434th Fighter Training Squadron "Red Devils" T-38C flies in 2007.

On October 1, 2007, the 47th Civil Engineer Squadron's housing flight stood down. Base housing from that time onward was overseen by Pinnacle-Hunt Housing as part of an Air Force–wide housing privatization effort, which removed base housing from military management to put it into private hands. This photograph shows a member of the base's Civil Engineer Squadron team doing an environmental inspection in 1995.

Also in 2007, on April 11, the Mission Support Squadron and Services Division merged into the 47th Force Support Squadron (Provisional) during a ceremony pictured here. This test would prove successful and lead to all such organizations across the Air Force merging into force support squadrons. Then, on December 2, 2011, the 47th Student Squadron was reactivated, allowing the 47th Operations Support Squadron to focus solely on managing the airfield.

In a first for Laughlin Air Force Base and the Afghanistan Air Force, three Afghanistan Air Force lieutenants graduated from SUPT at Laughlin on December 18, 2011. Their training at Laughlin followed a July 2007 visit to the base by Afghan general Muhammad Dawran (left), pictured here with wing commander Col. Edward M. Minahan during that summer's visit to the base.

On January 10, 2012, the Air Force Flight Standards Agency declared that Laughlin Air Force Base was the busiest Air Force base in the United States for 2011. Laughlin has consistently remained in the "top 10 busiest bases" overall. In this photograph, Laughlin personnel go on the radio to promote the base's 2012 Adventure Race.

On April 24, 2012, the 84th Flying Training Squadron was inactivated, and the 434th Fighter Training Squadron was redesignated the 434th Flying Training Squadron (434 FTS). Today, the 434 FTS helps share the load of the T-6 flying mission with the 85 FTS and the 96 FTS. This 2004 photograph shows Laughlin T-6s flying in formation.

Air Education and Training Command (AETC) announced on December 18, 2012, that the City of Del Rio had won the 2013 AETC Community Support Award (also called the Altus Trophy). This 2015 photograph depicts Laughlin's former main gate before it was moved in 2018 to the west gate, where it resides today.

On January 21, 2016, Laughlin Air Force Base began a new tradition with SUPT Class 16-04 with the inaugural, interfaith Blessing of the Wings. Participation in this religious ceremony is entirely optional, but it affords those who would like to participate an opportunity to better connect their faith to their flying. This photograph depicts a Laughlin class in 2005 posing before a wings display at Laughlin's Heritage Park.

On February 22, 2016, a disastrous thunder-, wind-, and hailstorm wreaked havoc across Laughlin. No one was hurt, but enormous damage was done to aircraft and infrastructure, as shown in this image of one of the base's houses. Flight ops resumed on February 25, but it took more than four years for all of the damage to be repaired. The last damaged T-1 airplane returned to Laughlin in December 2020.

On June 23, 2017, Laughlin broke ground for a new on-base STEM-focused elementary school. Classes began on August 20, 2018. In 2019, the school was named after Vietnam War vet and educator Bobby Barrera. In this picture from the school's dedication ceremony, wing commander Col. Lee G. Gentile Jr. (left) and school namesake Roberto "Bobby" Barrera (right) flank school board vice president Linda Guanajuato-Webb as she cuts the ribbon.

In the summer of 2019, the 47th Flying Training Wing began utilizing Virtual Reality (VR) technologies with its pilot training program, enhancing student learning with more realistic simulations and virtual hands-on practice. Although this style of training is still in its infancy, it provides a much more realistic version of the time-tested "chair flying" of days passed, where students would mentally map out their flight plans in their heads.

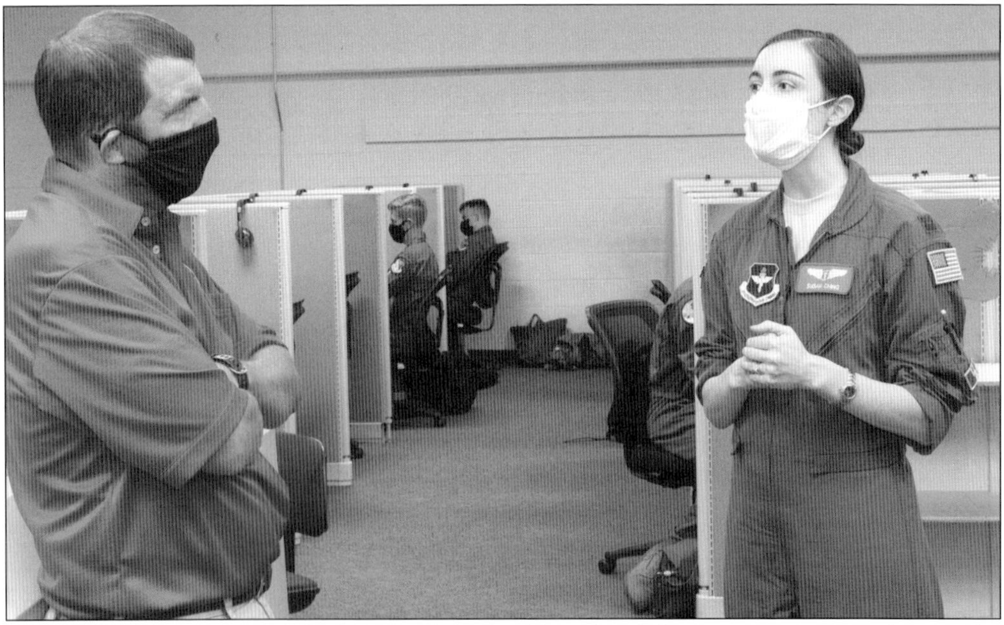

In 2020, Laughlin, along with the rest of the world, endured the COVID-2019 pandemic. The challenge was to continue producing pilots while keeping personnel healthy. Capt. Susan Ching, a doctor with 47 FTW Public Health, helped, with others in the 47th Medical Group, lead the wing's response to the pandemic. She is pictured here (right) speaking with 47th Operations Group's T-6 lead civilian simulator instructor, Jim DeReus, about COVID-19 precautions.

Seven

Laughlin Air Force Base

Air Park and Heritage

In the previous six chapters, this book described the chronological history of Laughlin Air Force Base, tracing its story from when it was first established in 1942 to the time of this book's publication. This chapter, however, examines the physical history of Laughlin Air Force Base and what visitors to the base can find there.

Specifically, this chapter looks at the nine airplanes that make up the base's air park, plus a number of monuments, memorials, and buildings around the base that are worth visiting if one wishes to immerse themselves in the history and heritage of the facility at large. This chapter does not completely account for all of the heritage displays on the base. Many units, flights, and offices have individual heritage collections, hanging on their walls or on display, all throughout the base. These exhibits usually highlight the history of that particular organization, including its time at Laughlin Air Force Base, but also, for the flying squadrons in particular, showcasing their combat heritage from before they were reactivated at Laughlin Air Force Base.

This chapter only examines some of the major heritage displays on base (as of the publication of this book), including the air park, that are readily accessible to any visitor without requiring a tour or entrance to a specific building or office facility. Heritage is and always has been important to the military, and it is very likely that these exhibits will be added to in the future as the wing and the base continue to evolve and gain history over time.

This photograph of the old front gate from 1994 shows where one can find the nine static display aircraft that make up the Laughlin Air Force Base Heritage Air Park. As of the writing of this book, there are plans in development to move these airplanes from this location to the new main gate, but they have not come to fruition just yet. The main road pictured here, from the gate and down the middle of the base, is called Liberty Drive. Part of the reason the main gate was moved from this location to its present-day spot was due to the presence of the railroad tracks, seen at the bottom of this picture, which could present a safety hazard to drivers during the crowded morning hours when cars lined up outside the checkpoint to enter the base at the same time that a regularly scheduled morning train would be utilizing those tracks.

In 1952, the first of about 60 Republic F-84D Thunderjets arrived at Laughlin for use by the 3645th Combat Crew Training Wing, which provided transition training for newly graduated pilots going to F-84s or F-86s. The airplane pictured here is actually an upgraded version called the F-84F Thunderstreak and has little resemblance to the straight-winged predecessor actually flown on the base (but which are very rare today).

The placard that goes with the F-84 tells the story of a Laughlin graduate, Eugene H. Fisher. A couple of firsts are also attributed to the F-84: it was the first fighter plane capable of in-flight refueling, and it was the first single-seat fighter capable of carrying a tactical nuclear weapon.

Seeing the need for a jet trainer, Lockheed engineers stretched the F-80's (the first US Air Force jet to see combat) airframe to add a second cockpit. Initially designated the TP-80, the Air Force redesignated the aircraft as the Lockheed T-33A Shooting Star, pictured here, and ordered it as an advanced trainer. Up until the late 1950s, the aircraft even retained two .50-caliber machine guns.

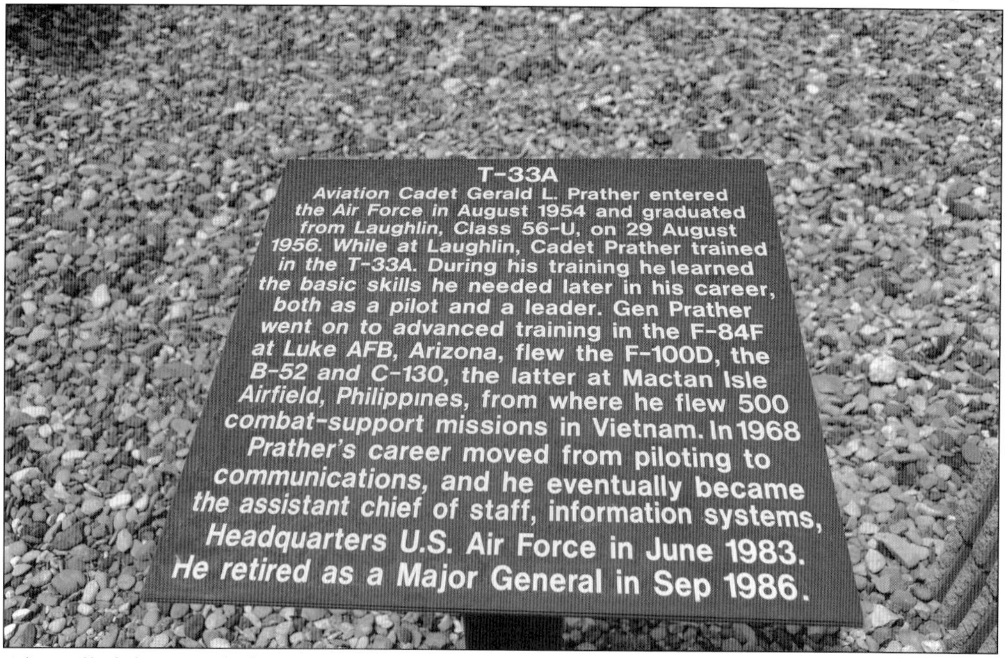

Also called the T-Bird, this aircraft came to Laughlin in 1952 when the base came back on active status to train US and Allied pilots during the Korean War. One of the pilots who trained on this aircraft, Gen. Gerald Prather, whose career is described here, actually retired to Del Rio, Texas, and became one of the base's biggest supporters. There is even a road on base named after him.

Before gaining fame as the producer of the P-51 and B-25, North American was known primarily for its training aircraft. The AT-6 Texan (for "advanced trainer"), pictured here, is one such example. Between 1939 and 1945, North American produced over 15,000 Texans. AT-6s served at Laughlin in 1944–1945. Today, Laughlin pilots first learn how to fly on the Beechcraft T-6 Texan II, named in honor of this first "pilot maker" plane.

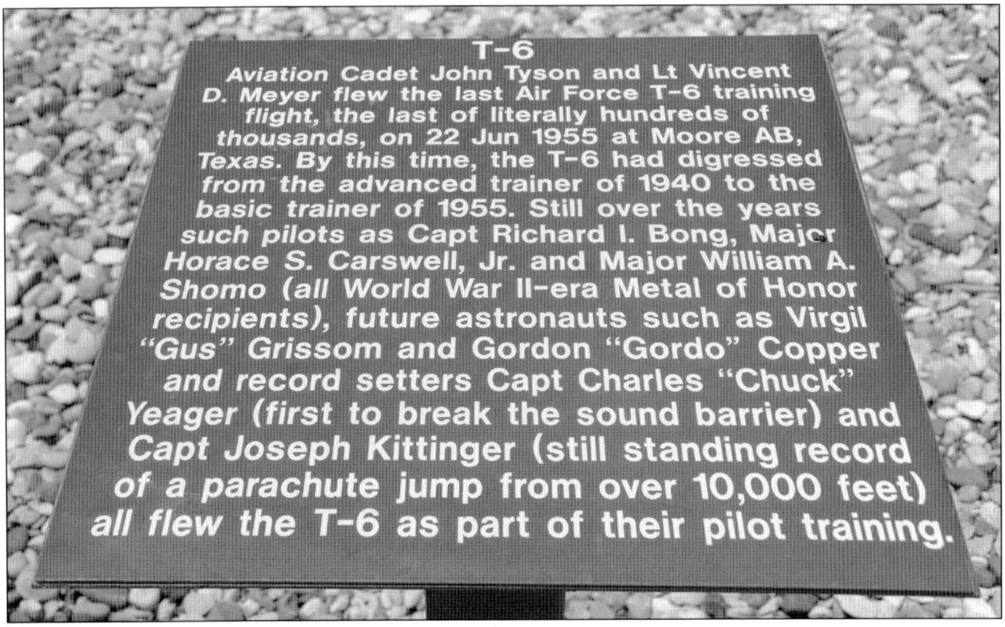

Please note that this placard has a typographical error: It should say "from over 100,000 feet" at the bottom, not "10,000 feet." Capt. Joseph Kittinger's record-shattering jump has actually been beaten now as well, most recently by Robert Alan Eustace (2014). Another fun fact, however, is that British Commonwealth pilots who underwent flight school in Canada also flew on the T-6, which they called the Harvard.

In 1948, the Air Force sought a replacement for the T-6 Texan and solicited designs. North American won the competition, producing the North American T-28A Trojan, pictured here. Seeing that most aircraft then had a tricycle landing gear (versus being a tail-dragger like the T-6), engineers designed the Trojan with that style of undercarriage from the beginning. The first XT-28 flew in September 1949, and production started in 1950.

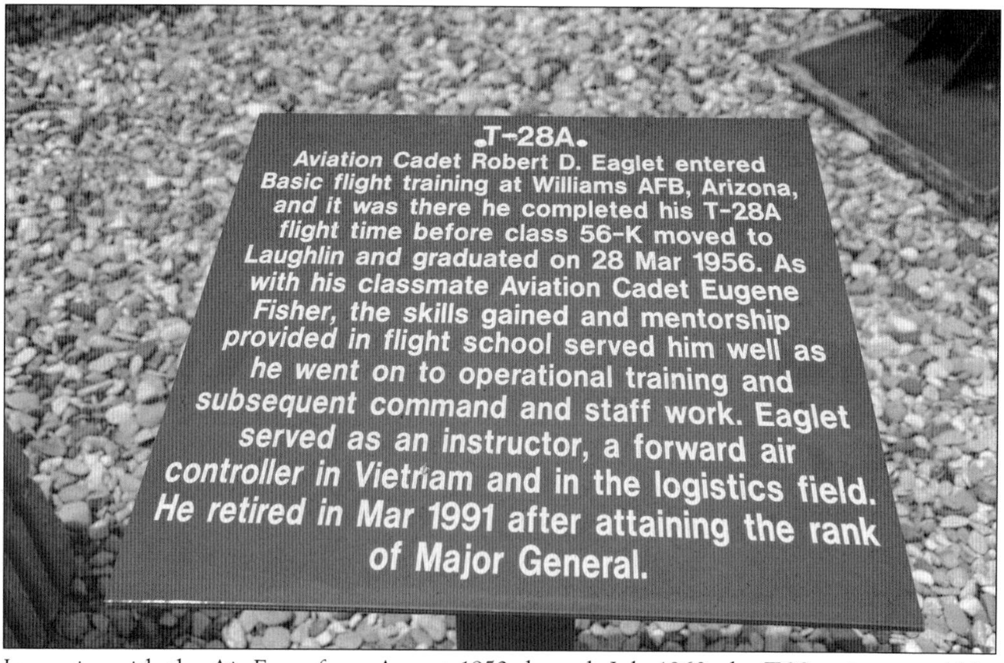

In service with the Air Force from August 1950 through July 1960, the T-28 trainers could be fitted with armament, including two .50-caliber machine guns, two 100-pound bombs, or six 2.25-inch rockets, but they seldom were. The mission placard accompanying this static display, pictured here, talks about one of the pilots from Laughlin who flew in this plane.

Design started on the Douglas A-26 Invader before America's entry into World War II, and the aircraft entered service in 1944. The fastest attack aircraft of the period, Army Air Force leaders chose the A-26 to replace both the A-20 and B-26. Since B-26 crews trained at Laughlin, the base started converting to the A-26 in December 1944. This particular airplane is an A-26C but has been modified to represent an A-26B.

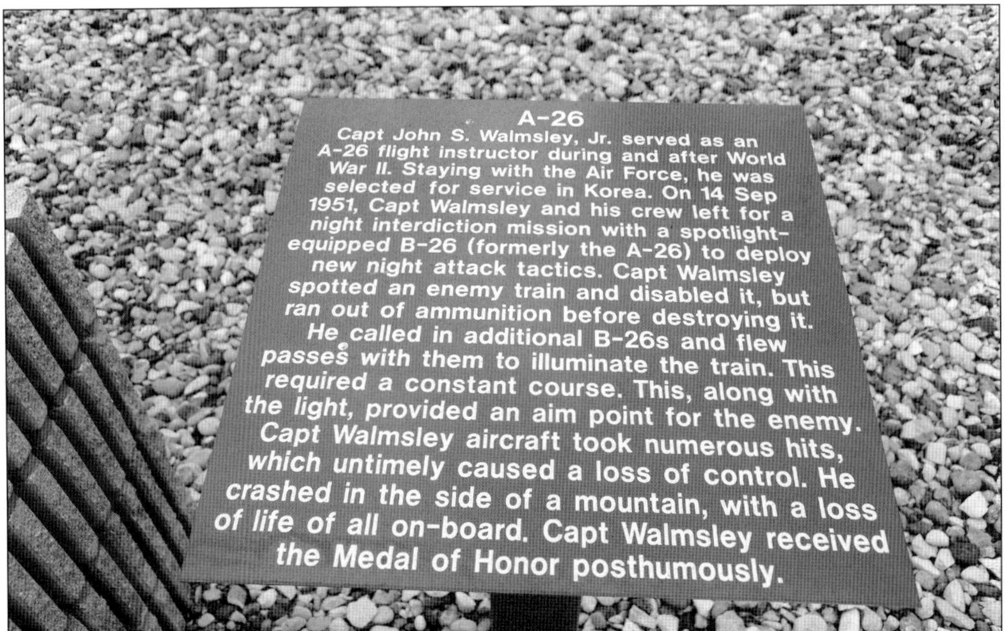

The Invader went on to serve in Korea (as the B-26) and Vietnam as the A-26K and flew its last combat mission, a night-interdiction sortie over the Ho Chi Minh Trail, on November 9, 1969. The mission placard accompanying this display, photographed here, describes the career of Invader pilot Capt. John S. Walmsley Jr., who was awarded the Medal of Honor.

In 1950, the Air Force looked for a tactical bomber to replace the Douglas A-26 (by now the B-26). With solicitation narrowed to the Martin XB-51 and English Electric's Canberra, the Air Force held a fly-off competition, with the British design the winner. The EB-57B on display at Laughlin, pictured here, bears a strong resemblance to the RB-57Cs utilized by Laughlin's 4080th Strategic Reconnaissance Wing.

This mission placard discusses the noteworthy career of Col. Hubert Zemke, the commander who brought the 4080th Strategic Reconnaissance Wing to Laughlin and helped to lead it as it settled into the base. During World War II, his 56th Fighter Group, famously known as Zemke's Wolf Pack, aided the Allies in winning the war in Europe.

The 4080th Strategic Reconnaissance Wing (later the 4080th Strategic Wing) was the only Air Force unit equipped with the U-2A during the 1950s and early 1960s, and pilots from this unit performed the overflights of Cuba during the missile crisis using CIA U-2Cs like this one. The U-2C was fitted with an updated engine for higher altitudes and possessed larger air intakes than the A model.

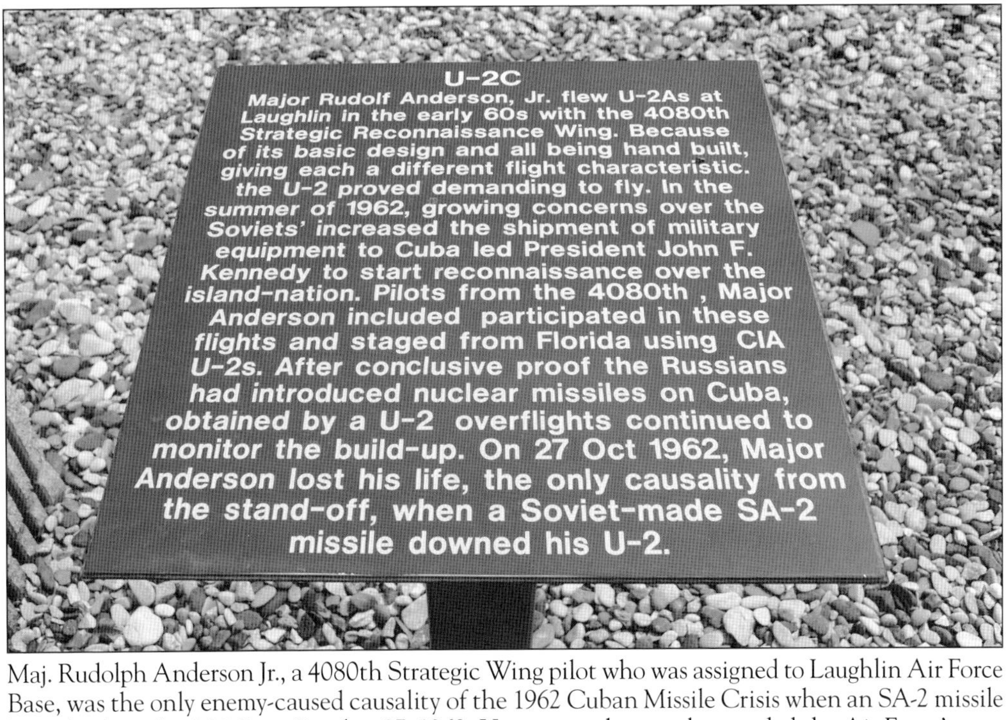

Maj. Rudolph Anderson Jr., a 4080th Strategic Wing pilot who was assigned to Laughlin Air Force Base, was the only enemy-caused causality of the 1962 Cuban Missile Crisis when an SA-2 missile brought down his U-2C on October 27, 1962. He was posthumously awarded the Air Force's very first Air Force Cross, and Laughlin's Anderson Hall is named in his honor.

At the same time the Air Force requested designs that led to the T-28, it also solicited proposals for a new basic trainer. Beech won the competition with its T-34 Mentor. No T-34s served at Laughlin, but this aircraft is on display at the base. The aircraft on display is actually a Navy T-34B, too, though the only difference was in the instrumentation.

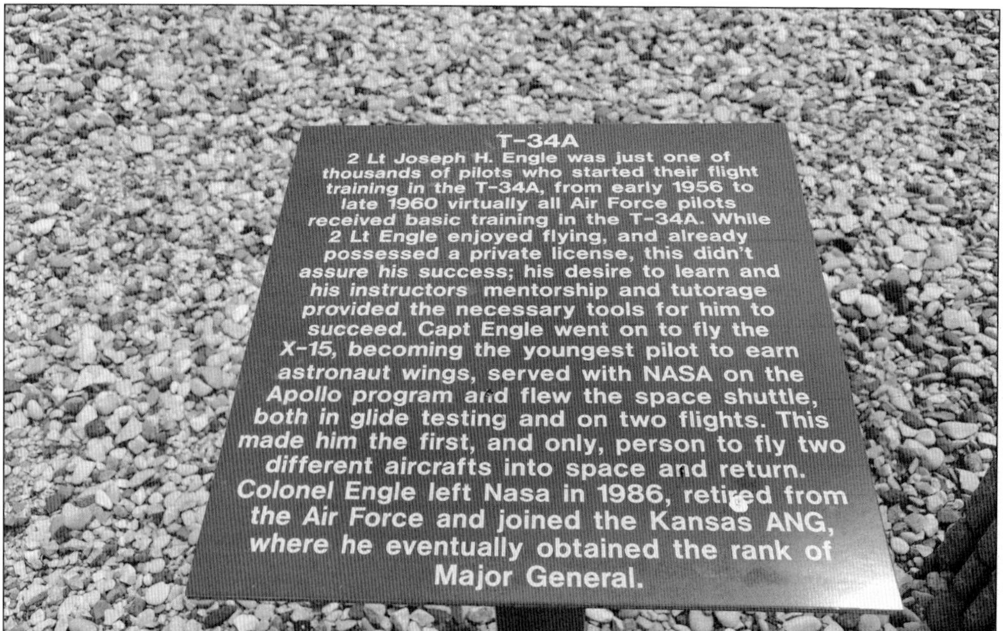

The mission placard pictured here describes the career of NASA astronaut Joseph H. Engle, who learned to fly on a T-34 Mentor. Although Engle did not get his wings at Laughlin Air Force Base, a number of NASA astronauts did, including Curtis L. Brown Jr. and Mark C. Lee. NASA still utilizes the T-38, which is also flown at Laughlin.

In 1940, Beech started building the C-45 and three trainer versions: the AT-7 (navigation), the AT-10 (twin-engine pilot), and the AT-11 (bombardier and aerial gunner). The C-45 version primarily provided transportation but could be used for light cargo or communication work. AT-7s and AT-11s served at Laughlin in 1944–1945, while a UC-45G and H served at various times between 1953 and 1958. The aircraft on display is actually a Navy SNB-5, though.

The mission placard for Laughlin's C-45 describes Col. Thomas Mosley's time commanding at Laughlin (1952–1955) and the ways in which these aircraft were utilized. Because they had no official role in training pilots, the C-45s were primarily used for transport of personnel and supplies. This allowed for air travel without requiring that a training plane be taken away from its training mission for it.

The T-38 is the only display aircraft at Laughlin that is still being actively flown there. This aircraft, with a T-37 Tweet, can be found at the Ribas-Dominicci Plaza in the traffic circle just beyond the base's main gate. In 2019, following their deaths in training accidents in 2017 and 2018 respectively, the names of Capt. Paul "Stuck" Barbour and Capt. John "Trojan" Graziano were added to this plane in tribute.

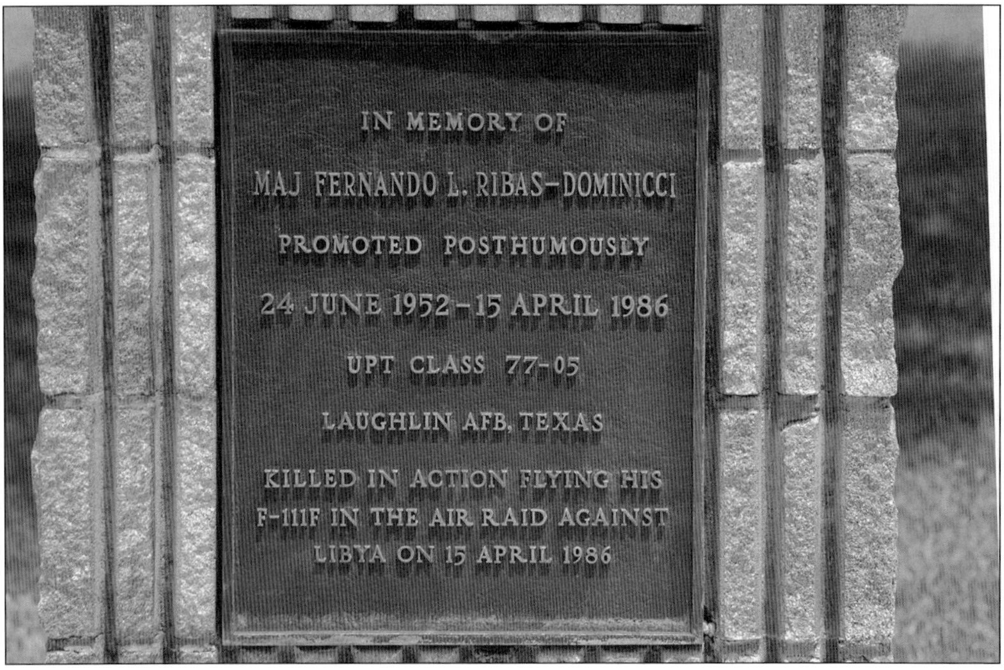

The Ribas-Dominicci Plaza is dedicated to Maj. Fernando L. Ribas-Dominicci, who lost his life in the 1986 raid against Libya. The raid against Libya was in response to state-sponsored terrorism and was targeted against identified terrorist training camps. Major Ribas-Dominicci was serving with the 48th Tactical Fighter Wing when his F-111F Aardvark was shot down, killing both him and his weapons systems officer, Capt. Paul F. Lorence.

The Cessna T-37 Tweet was Laughlin's primary trainer until 2004, when it was fully replaced by the T-6 flown today. This display aircraft can be found in the Ribas-Dominicci Plaza and bears the name of Capt. Drew Kajans. Captain Kajans, an instructor pilot at Laughlin with the 96th Flying Training Squadron, died in 2001. The aircraft was dedicated in his memory at a ceremony on June 18, 2002.

This image captured the crowd at the ceremony on June 18, 2002, when the T-37 display plane was dedicated in memory of Capt. Drew Kajans. In attendance in the first row, fourth from the left, was his surviving spouse, Trina Ann Kajans, and one of his two daughters beside her. His other daughter is who the crowd is watching as she performs a musical tribute to her father.

In September 2005, a ceremony was held dedicating the Laughlin Air Force Base fitness center in the name of A1C Raymond Losano. Airman First Class Losano was never stationed at Laughlin, but he was a native of Del Rio, Texas. He served as a tactical air command and control specialist during Operation Enduring Freedom in Afghanistan, where he was killed by injuries he received in combat on April 25, 2003.

Attending the ceremony were Raymond Losano's parents and family, including his wife, Sarah, and two children, pictured here beside wing commander Col. Tod D. Wolters. For his actions, which ended with him being mortally wounded—but not before he was able to call in the air support that saved his ambushed unit—he was posthumously awarded the Bronze Star with Valor and the Purple Heart.

In addition to the Losano Fitness Center, a number of buildings are named in honor of Air Force veterans or Laughlin personnel. The Operations Group's headquarters is the Jarvis Building, named in honor of Chief Master Sergeant Daniel P. Jarvis. The dedication of the building is highlighted on this interior display inside the structure's front entrance.

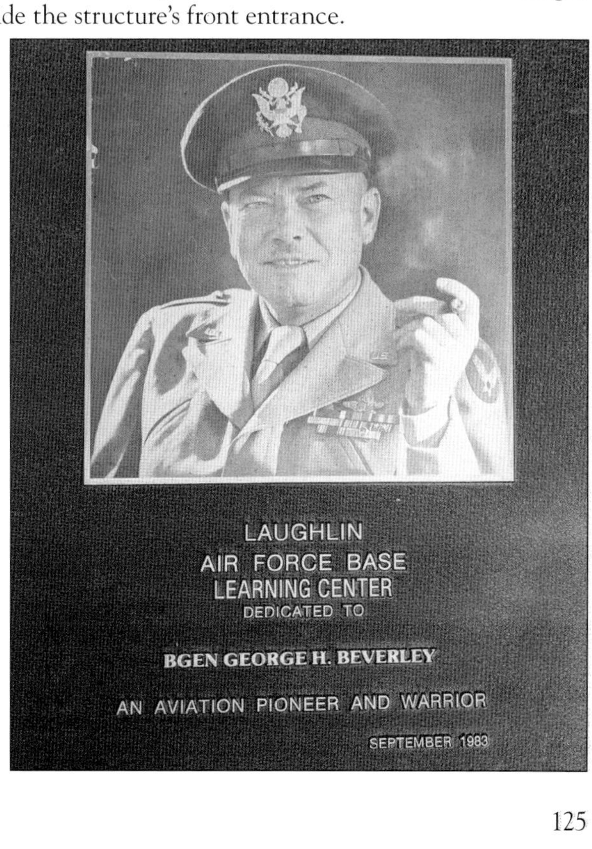

In addition to the building being named after Chief Jarvis, the Operations Group's computer lab is dedicated in honor of Brig. Gen. George H. Beverley, pictured here. Originally, the education center was memorialized in General Beverley's name in 1983, but after it was torn down, the computer aided instruction lab was dedicated in its place. General Beverley fought in both world wars and was a pioneer of military aviation.

Another building dedicated to someone who served or helped Laughlin Air Force Base is Pritchett Hall, named in memory of Shirley M. Pritchett, who worked at Laughlin for 35 years. Other buildings that have been memorialized and mentioned in other parts of this book include Anderson Hall and Ricks Hall.

Although Laughlin's primary mission has been training pilots for many decades, its permanent personnel do deploy. This memorial stone, which the Laughlin Heritage Foundation helped to make possible, remembers some of those from Laughlin who lost their lives in the Vietnam War. In the past, in the present, and in the future, America's military stands ever ready to defend the nation.

INDEX